D0764508

Microsoft

Project 2013 Plain & Simple

Ben Howard

Published with the authorization of Microsoft Corporation by:
O'Reilly Media, Inc.
1005 Gravenstein Highway North
Sebastopol, California 95472

ISBN: 978-0-7356-7199-7

1 2 3 4 5 6 7 8 9 QG 8 7 6 5 4 3

Printed and bound in the United States of America.

Microsoft Press books are available through booksellers and distributors worldwide. If you need support related to this book, email Microsoft Press Book Support at mspinput@microsoft.com. Please tell us what you think of this book at *http://www.microsoft.com/learning/booksurvey.*

Acquisitions and Developmental Editor: Kenyon Brown
Production Editor: Melanie Yarbrough
Editorial Production: Box Twelve Communications
Technical Reviewer: Ellen Lehnert
Copyeditor: nSight, Inc.
Indexer: Judith McConville
Cover Design: Twist Creative • Seattle
Cover Composition: Karen Montgomery
Illustrator: Kara Ebrahim

For Andrea, Libby, and Maria

Contents

Acknowledgments

Many thanks to Kenyon Brown for giving me the opportunity to write this book; Melanie Yarbrough for guiding the book through production; and copy editor Chris Norton and many others in the extended O'Reilly team for their ability to turn my jumble of words into something worthy of publishing. Finally, a big thanks goes to Ellen Lehnert for her excellent technical review.

About this book

1

If you've opened this book and have started reading this paragraph, chances are that you're running a project, or you have one to run, and you're interested in learning how to use Microsoft Project 2013 to help you manage it. You might already have had some experience using Project, either this version or an earlier one, or you might have used a tool such as Microsoft Excel to create a task list and produce a Gantt chart and this is your first experience of Project. It could be that you've seen other people using Project in a way that has saved them time, allowed them to accurately track their projects, and enabled them to produce professional-looking reports.

Whatever has drawn you to this book, *Microsoft Project 2013 Plain & Simple*, I've written it in a way that explains how to set up, track, and report on a project, allowing you to get to work immediately. My goal in writing this book was two-fold. First, for users who have never used Project before, I wanted to provide a concise and simple way to build a project schedule that puts them in control. Second, for users who have used Project before, I wanted to unravel some of the complexities associated with using it by providing clear and concise instructions to perform specific tasks.

In this section:

- No computerese!
- A quick overview
- A few assumptions
- What's new in Project 2013?
- Using a touch-enabled system
- A final few words

No computerese!

This is a book about Project and how to begin to get the most out of it. No task in this book makes you read more than two pages to find an answer to your question. Look up what you need to do in the table of contents or index, follow the steps in the task, and you're done. If there are several ways to achieve the same goal (and often there are in Project), I'll try to list them and then show you step by step how to achieve the goal, using one of the methods listed. Often there isn't always a right way or a wrong way of achieving a task, and one of my continual delights of Project is finding a different way to achieve the same outcome.

A large part of the success of working with Project lies in setting up the right view of the data, at the right time, in order to complete your task. Because this is a recurring theme, I vary the steps used to set up the view. I want to ensure that you are not afraid to explore and use Project to its full potential!

Like many (or all) Microsoft products, Project comes with its own set of terms and concepts. In several sections I've taken the opportunity to expand on and explain the terms and concepts, where relevant, in order to help you get the most out of Project.

A project plan, or schedule, is just a model, or representation, of the actual project you are going to run. Projects vary in length from days to years, from the simple to the complex. What you decide to build using Project depends very much on exactly what information you need to track and manage. For this book I build a project plan for creating a new product, and the same plan gets added to during each section. The plan is based upon a real project, so you can be sure that everything you see in this book is tried and tested in real life.

When starting to use Project, it can appear to be a complex and daunting tool. When writing the book and taking the screen shots, I used all of the default settings, so what you see in the screen shots, and the steps I describe, will be the ones that you will perform to achieve the same goal. The screen shots were taken at a resolution of 1024 × 768, so because Project will resize the icons on the ribbon for different screen resolutions, your ribbon might be slightly different.

With this release of Project, there are now three different versions of Project. *Project Standard* and *Project Professional* are the two base versions, and differ slightly in some additional functionality (these differences are noted in the book where applicable). *Project Pro for Office 365* is the same software as Project Professional 2013, it is just licensed and distributed via a subscription service. You can find your version by accessing the Account tab within the Backstage area.

This book is based on Microsoft Project 2013 Professional installed on the Microsoft Windows 7 operating system, but if you are using Windows 8, you'll find that everything works just the same.

I've tried to create as many Tips as possible, simply because the more you know about a tool, the quicker you become the master of it. I've also added in a few Cautions to keep you on the right track and the occasional See Also.

A quick overview

The sections in this book are organized logically for the types of tasks you'll want to achieve or perform using Project. If you are new to Project, you can start at the beginning and work your way through the relevant sections for your project. If you've used Project before but just want to brush up on some techniques or find the easiest way to accomplish something, then just browse the relevant section or task and get started.

Every project, from the simplest to the most complex, follows a basic "project life cycle." During different phases of the life cycle, you use different features of Project to enable you to run your project as smoothly and efficiently as possible.

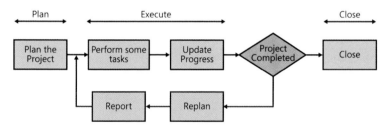

The sections in this book, and the ordering of the sections, are based loosely on the project life cycle shown in the diagram.

Section 2, entitled "Getting started with Project 2013," helps you understand some of the terms used in Project, how to navigate and use the interface, and how to change the interface so that the data displayed is exactly what you need to have displayed. As someone who is running a project, you might be spending a lot of time using Project, so it makes sense to learn your way around it.

Section 3, "Getting the Project basics right," talks you through some fundamental settings that you should think about and set before you start building your plan. Doing this before you create the tasks will save a lot of heartache later on. Once these items are set, you're good to save the plan.

Section 4, "Creating and modifying tasks," teaches you how to create and build a complete "Work Breakdown Structure" fully representing all of the tasks you need to perform in order to complete the project.

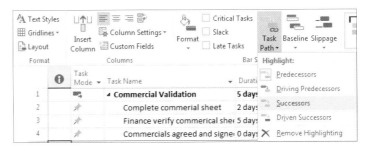

Section 5, "Setting estimates," discusses the difference between duration and work and how to set and enter estimates for each task. Providing realistic and defensible estimates for tasks ensures that you will have a realistic chance of achieving them.

Section 6, "Linking the tasks," helps you understand how to link tasks together so that you can set the correct order in which the tasks need to be completed. Once tasks are sequenced together, it's possible to view the task path and determine how long the whole project will take.

Section 7, "Assigning and managing resources," discusses what types of resources you can use in Project, how to create them, and how to assign them to tasks. Project uses three types of resources: Work, Material, and Cost.

Section 8, "Adding external dependencies and deadlines," helps you apply and review the consequences of any items that can affect your project but are outside of your control.

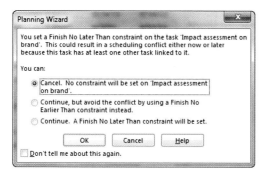

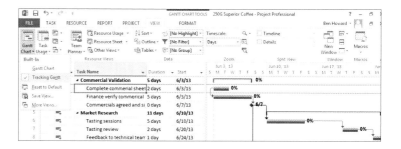

Section 9, "Communicating the plan," is all about producing great looking reports and presentations right out of Project. Producing a monthly status report has never been so easy.

Section 11, "Closing the project," works through what to do at the end of the project. Is everything complete? What lessons can you learn from this project? Can you use the project as a template to make the next project better?

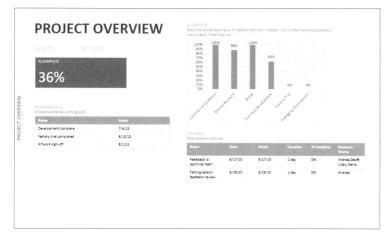

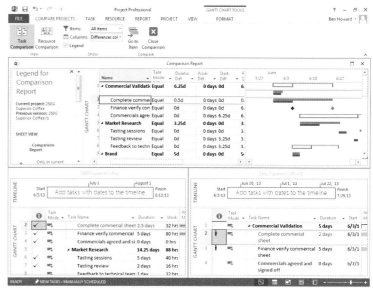

Section 10, "Updating and replanning," deals with how to track the progress of the project. When you know what you need to do and you track what you actually did, you have a pretty good idea of what remains.

A few assumptions

When I run training courses on Project, I assume my delegates are computer literate and willing to learn—nothing else. They are attending a training course to learn how to use Project, and so they are either currently running a project or have been given the opportunity to run one. The majority of people I train don't have the job title of "Project Manager." Often they are doing other jobs that involve an element of project management, from an office move to an IT implementation, an engineering project to building a school. I can't begin to classify the different types of industries or the varieties of projects I've seen, talked about, and ultimately (in a small way) helped plan during those courses. I've assumed the readers of this book fall into that category.

What's new in Project 2013?

Project 2013 builds on the new features that were introduced in Project 2010, namely the ribbon and manually scheduled tasks. Microsoft didn't stand still, though, and completely rewrote the reporting within this version (removing the reports that first appeared in the very earliest versions of Project). They also provided some additional nifty features, such as the ability to easily see the sequence of tasks through the project. Along with the rest of the Microsoft Office products, Project now integrates seamlessly with your Microsoft account, letting you save documents to your SkyDrive or, if you have one, you can synchronize tasks to a Microsoft SharePoint server task list, providing easy collaboration within a project team no matter how geographically dispersed they are. Finally, if you are using Windows 8 and a touch device, you can begin to let your fingers do the talking.

Using a touch-enabled system

In this book I provide instructions based on traditional keyboard and mouse input methods. If you're using Project on a touch-enabled device, you might be giving commands by tapping with your finger or with a stylus. If so, substitute a tapping action any time I instruct you to click a user interface element. Also note that when I tell you to enter information in Project, you can do so by typing on a keyboard, tapping in the entry field under discussion to display and use the onscreen keyboard or even speaking aloud, depending on your computer setup and your personal preferences.

A final few words

I hope you find this book both informative and helpful; I wrote it because I've met many people who struggled with Project and I wanted to demystify the art of using it. I think Project is a fabulous tool, and I hope that by using this book you will too.

Getting started with Project 2013

2

It is very easy to create a great looking Gantt chart with Microsoft Project 2013, but in order to really utilize the power of Project 2013 you should spend some time getting familiar with the user interface, the different views that Project uses to display information, and the difference between project, task, resource, and assignment information.

Understanding Project terminology

If you are new to Project, I'm afraid you are going to need to learn some new terminology, and I'm sorry to say that there really is no getting away from it! The good news is that once you have learned this terminology, it will enhance your understanding when you read this book and it will enhance your use of Project.

The terms I want to introduce you to first are project, task, resource, and assignment.

A project is a temporary group activity designed to produce a unique product, service, or result (the outcome). From a Project perspective, a project is the plan that you create which details how you, or your organization, will go about creating the desired outcome.

The project plan is comprised of a set of tasks. A single task represents a single "thing" that needs to be completed; the complete list of tasks completely defines what needs to be done in order to achieve the outcome. Therefore, if all the tasks are completed successfully, the project outcome will be achieved. So a task represents a single "thing" to complete, and the list of tasks represents the full list of "things to do."

In order to complete the tasks, you will need one or more resources. From a Project perspective, a resource is something you use to get tasks done, so resources can be people, machinery, materials, or money.

If the task list defines what is to be done and the resource list defines the resources you have at your disposal, then an assignment is the allocation of a resource to a task. From a Project perspective this would be termed "resource assignment," and an example would be assigning the "Project Manager" to the task "Define Business Case."

SEE ALSO For more definitions, go the Project Management Institute (PMI) website at *http://www.pmi.org/About-Us/About-Us-What-is-Project-Management.aspx*.

Understanding how tasks and resources relate to each other

A Microsoft Project Plan file (.mpp) is really just a database (it's actually possible to open up the .mpp file in Microsoft Access). Project contains four entities—Project, Task, Resource, and Assignments—so although you do not need to understand the relationships between the entities in depth, you should attempt to understand the following high-level diagram:

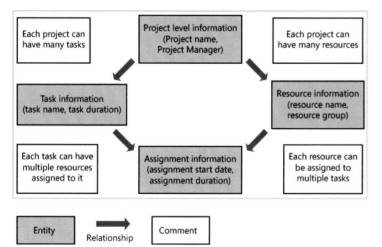

Understanding the different entities and the relationships between them will help you use the correct view when looking at project data—for example, if you wanted to look at task information, you would need to choose a task-centric view or table (Gantt Chart, Tracking Gantt, and so on). Resource information is shown using a view or table, such as the Resource Sheet or the Resource Graph. Assignment information is shown by selecting the Resource Usage view or the Task Usage view.

Project level information is information that applies to the entire project, such as the Project Start Date and the Project Calendar(s). This information is viewed in different areas depending upon the type of data held. Project level information is available in the Project Information area on the Backstage (don't worry, I explain what the Backstage is later in this section), and within that the Project Statistics and Advanced Properties windows. Information such as the project's Start Date, Duration, and other schedule-related information is available in the Project Summary Task (again, don't worry; I explain what the Project Summary Task is later in this section).

Navigating Microsoft Project

When you start Project, you are prompted to open an existing project or a new project. If you open a previously saved project, the project is opened in the same view that was displayed when you saved it.

The Project screen is split into several areas, and it's important to be able to recognize the areas in order to successfully navigate around the Project interface. As you use Project, you'll find that not all views use all areas. The default view is the Gantt With Timeline view, so I will use this view to describe the screen.

- The Quick Access Toolbar and Ribbon

- The Timeline

- The Table Area

- The Chart Area

- The Status Bar

The ribbon and the Quick Access Toolbar provide access to the main functions and features of Project, replacing the menu structure that existed prior to Project 2010.

The Quick Access Toolbar appears at the top of the screen, and it provides single-click access to your favorite commands. You can customize the Toolbar by selecting the drop-down menu to the right of the Toolbar, which then allows you to add or remove commands. The menu also allows you to place the Toolbar below the ribbon.

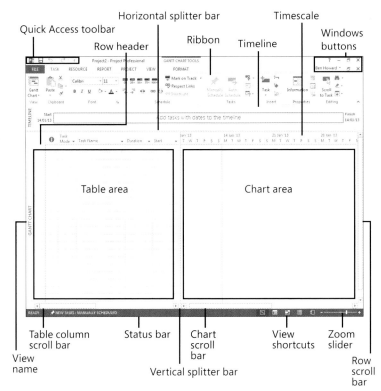

The ribbon is composed of seven tabs (File, Task, Resource, Report, Project, View, and Format), and each tab contains a set of buttons and commands that are relevant to the tab—for example, all of the File buttons and commands exist on the File tab. Each set of commands on the ribbon is grouped together—for example, all of the buttons required to create new tasks are within the Insert group on the Tasks tab. You can customize the ribbon by right-clicking it and selecting Customize The Ribbon, or you can hide it by selecting Collapse The Ribbon.

The Timeline shows a "bird's eye view" of the key stages and tasks of the project plan, which can then be shared through other office applications, such as Microsoft Outlook or Microsoft PowerPoint. As a user, you decide which tasks appear on the Timeline, and as the project schedule changes, the dates for the tasks on the Timeline change automatically. The Timeline has multiple format options to enable you to select the fonts, font sizes, colors, and so on, and tasks can be rearranged on the Timeline to ensure that they are easy to view. Finally, when the Timeline is pasted into another application, the components of the Timeline are pasted as individual Office Art Shapes, enabling further formatting. The Timeline is separated from the main view by the horizontal splitter bar.

The Table area is split into rows and columns, like a worksheet. Within the Gantt Chart view, each row contains a task and each column contains a specific piece of information about the task. Task columns can be hidden (but not deleted), and additional task columns can be inserted. Use the scroll bars (horizontal and vertical) to navigate up and down the task list or left and right within the Table area to see additional columns.

The Chart area is shown to the right of the table and displays for each task a bar representing the duration of each task based upon the start and finish dates of the task. The bars within the Chart area can display other information, such as Percent Complete or Resource Names. Vertical lines mark the current date, project start date, and project finish date. The timescale indicates the current timeframe shown in the Chart area (by default, this is set to "days").

The Status bar appears at the bottom of the window and displays the task mode for New Tasks (Manually Scheduled or Auto Scheduled), shortcuts to different views, and the Zoom Slider. The Zoom Slider alters the Timescale.

The Table area and Chart area are divided by the vertical splitter bar. This bar can be moved to the left or right to display more of the table or chart area as desired.

Understanding the Backstage view

The ribbon contains the set of commands for working on a project schedule, while the Backstage view contains the set of commands you use to do things to a project schedule.

To access the Backstage view, click the File tab. The Backstage view is where you manage your projects and related data about them—create, save, and share documents, print them, view the project properties and account information, set options such as

the default view, and more. The commands within the Backstage view are shown as a menu structure, and clicking on a command displays further options within the main body of the view—for example, choosing the Print option provides access to printer settings and shows a print preview.

To return to your project from the Backstage view, click the large back arrow button.

Access the Backstage view

1 Click the File tab.

2 Review the Options within the Backstage view.

3 To exit the Backstage view, click the back arrow.

TIP To quickly exit the Backstage view, press the Esc key.

Understanding the ribbon

The ribbon is the main interface for accessing and using the features in Project, and it is composed of tabs, buttons, and commands. The seven tabs within Project are File, Task, Resource, Report, Project, View, and Format.

Click a tab to view and select the required buttons and commands related to the tab—for example, all the buttons and commands in the Task tab are related to tasks. On a tab, buttons and commands that are related in functionality are grouped together on the ribbon, and the name of the group is shown at the bottom of the ribbon. If there are too many buttons and commands to fit within a group, the ribbon displays an icon with a drop-down list that provides access to the hidden buttons. When additional options are available within a group, a small down arrow ⬐ (known as the dialog launcher) is displayed at the lower right-hand corner of the group; clicking on this arrow displays a dialog box showing the additional options.

The ribbon is both context sensitive and dynamic; buttons will be enabled or disabled depending on where you last clicked. If a button is enabled it will be "lit up" and you can click it. If it is disabled it will be dimmed and you can't click it. The size of the buttons and exactly what is displayed in the ribbon changes depending upon the screen resolution; a higher screen resolution is able to display larger buttons and more information than a lower screen resolution. The screen resolution used for screen shots in this book is 1024 × 768; your ribbon might look different depending upon your monitor's screen resolution.

You can customize the ribbon to your own requirements and export the customizations to other PCs.

Adding commands to the ribbon

Project has far too many commands to fit them all onto the ribbon. If you find your favorite commands are not available, or you want to add your own macros to the ribbon, you will need to customize it. You can't make changes to existing groups within the ribbon. All commands added to the ribbon will need to be added to a custom group, so the first task is to create one.

Add a command

1 Right-click the ribbon and select Customize The Ribbon.

2 Select the Tab name that you want the Custom Group to be part of.

3 Click New Group.

(continued on next page)

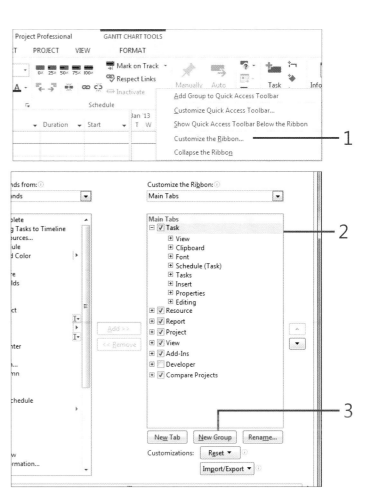

TIP Set your screen to the maximum resolution possible to provide the best view of the ribbon.

TIP Customizations to the ribbon can be exported to a file to enable you to move your configuration from one computer to another, or they can be reset by using the Reset button within the Customize The Ribbon dialog box.

Add a command *(continued)*

4 Select New Group (Custom) and click Rename.

5 Rename the custom group by overtyping your chosen group name and click OK.

6 Use the Choose commands from the option list to select your category of commands.

7 Select the command to add to the ribbon.

8 Click Add.

9 Click OK.

10 The command now appears on the ribbon.

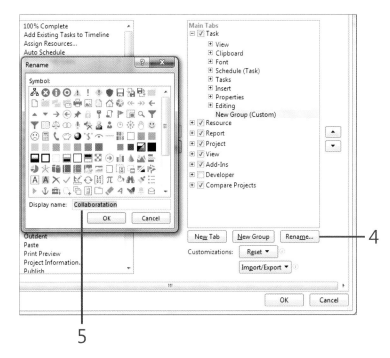

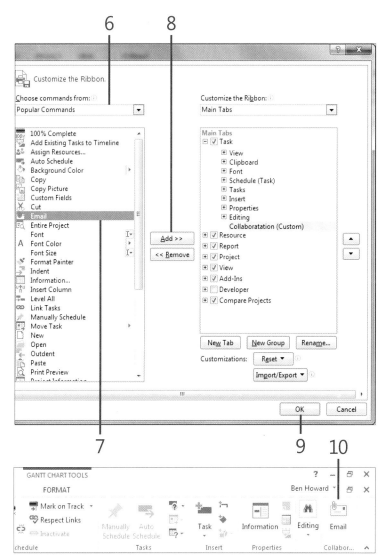

Collapsing and pinning the ribbon

The ribbon can be collapsed, which provides more room for viewing the project. When the ribbon is collapsed, the tabs remain displayed; clicking on a tab temporarily displays the ribbon, enabling you to select the commands. Pinning the ribbon back provides immediate and full access to the buttons and commands.

There are four ways to collapse the ribbon, and each method has a corresponding method to pin it back.

Collapse the ribbon	Pin the ribbon
Click the Collapse The Ribbon icon (⌃)	Click the Pin The Ribbon icon (⇥)
Right-click the ribbon and select Collapse the Ribbon	Right-click the ribbon and clear Collapse the Ribbon
Press Ctrl+F1	Press Ctrl+F1
Double-click a tab	Double-click a tab

Collapse and pin the ribbon

1   Click the Collapse The Ribbon icon on the right-hand side of the ribbon.

(continued on next page)

Collapse and pin the ribbon *(continued)*

2 The ribbon is hidden, and the tab names are displayed.

3 Double-click the Task tab to pin the ribbon.

4 The ribbon is displayed.

TIP Add the common commands you use to the Quick Access Toolbar; that way, those commands are readily available, even when the ribbon is collapsed.

TIP Collapse the ribbon when you want to display more of the chart area of the project; this is especially useful when working on a small computer screen.

Customizing the Quick Access Toolbar

The Quick Access Toolbar provides single-click access to commonly used commands and by default shows the Save, Undo, and Redo buttons. You can position the toolbar above or below the ribbon, and you can customize it by adding or removing commands from it.

Add a command to the Quick Access Toolbar

1 Click the drop-down menu list at the right of the Quick Access Toolbar.

2 Determine whether your required command is available on the menu. If it is, select it. If it isn't, select the More Commands menu option.

3 Select the command to add to the Quick Access Toolbar.

4 Click Add.

5 Click OK.

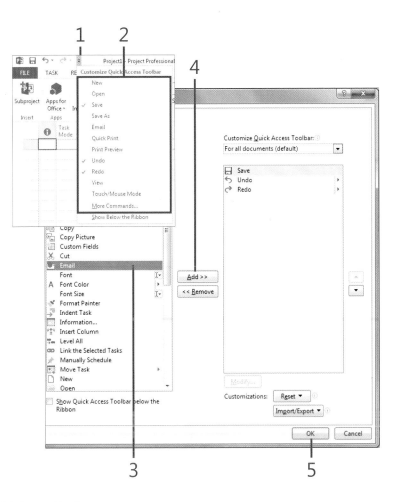

> **TIP**   Right-clicking any command on the ribbon gives an option to add the command to the Quick Access Toolbar. If you find you constantly use a command on the ribbon, this is by far the quickest and easiest way to add that command to the Quick Access Toolbar.

> **TRY THIS**   Add the Print Preview, Scroll to Task, Clear Filter, and Close commands to the toolbar.

Move the position of the Quick Access Toolbar

1 Click the drop-down menu list at the right of the Quick Access Toolbar.

2 Choose Show Below The Ribbon from the menu.

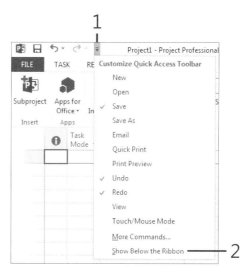

Understanding views, tables, filters, and groups

Project provides many ways to look at the schedule; these built-in ways are called views, and each view concentrates on a different aspect of the schedule. You use different views, tables, filters, and groups (a view is a combination of a table, filter, and group) to change the way Project presents the data to you. At different stages of a project, you will need to use different views in order to manage the project—for example, the information you want to present to team members regarding their tasks will be very different from the information you want to present to a customer at the end of a project.

You access the views from the Task, Resource, and View tabs, and because accessing different views is something that is done frequently, they appear as large buttons at the left-hand side of the ribbon.

There are three basic categories of views:

- Task
- Resource
- Assignment

Task-based views display information that is relative to tasks, such as the task name, duration, start date, finish date, and so on. Additionally, task-based views frequently provide a graphical representation of the tasks, such as a Gantt chart.

Resource-based views display information that is relative to resources, such as the resource name, the resource type, standard rate, and so on.

Assignment-based views display information that is relative to the assignment, such as the task name, task start date, task finish date, resource name, assignment start date, assignment finish date, and so on. Additionally, assignment-based views provide a timephased view of the scheduled work.

Each view comprises one or more of the following elements:

- A table
- A group
- A filter

A table appears to the left-hand side of the vertical splitter bar and is comprised of a set of columns relating to the entity (task, resource, or assignment). The table defines the columns displayed, the column order, the column width, the cell alignment, and so on. Project has many tables.

A group (or grouping) is used to combine or rearrange tasks or resources according to specific criteria—for example, active versus inactive tasks, task duration, and so on.

A filter is used to specify which tasks or resources should be displayed or highlighted within a view—for example, the Critical filter displays tasks that are on the critical path.

Project contains many views, tables, groups, and filters, and any one can be modified. If your modifications are very customized or specific, you might want to create new ones. Note that not all of the views contain a table or a group. Project has several built-in views that consist of a predefined form where a table is not valid.

The following table describes the more common views:

View Type	View Name	Description	Usage
Task	Gantt Chart	Displays common task columns and the Gantt chart.	Used to enter tasks.
	Gantt with Timeline	Displays the Timeline in the upper portion of the screen and the Gantt Chart view in the lower portion.	Used to place tasks on the Timeline. The Timeline view can be copied into other applications to help communicate the plan.
	Tracking Gantt	Displays common task columns and the Gantt chart; the Gantt chart is formatted to display Critical Tasks, the Baseline, and progress.	Used when the project is in progress and displays the variance between the baseline and the actual and planned duration.
Resource	Resource Sheet	Displays common resource columns.	Used to enter resources.
	Team Planner	Displays each resource and the tasks that the resource is assigned to.	Used to create and review assignments. Optionally used to reschedule tasks.
Assignment	Task Usage	Displays each task and the resources assigned to that task. In the right-hand portion of the screen, the work values are displayed.	Used for in-depth review of assignments, where the focus is primarily task-based.
	Resource Usage	Displays each resource and the tasks assigned to that resource. In the right-hand portion of the screen, the work values are displayed.	Used for in-depth review of assignments, where the focus is primarily resource-based.

 CAUTION   The Team Planner view and Inactive Tasks are available only in Project Professional.

Selecting a different view

Different views allow you to view different types of information, such as task information, resource information, or assignment information. Switching between views is so common in Project that Microsoft created a dedicated View tab, which not only provides easy access to different views, but also provides access to other commands and buttons that allow you to quickly change how you present the information within a view.

Select a different view

1 Click the View tab.

2 Click the Resource Sheet button.

3 Note that the view has changed, as shown by the view name.

(continued on next page)

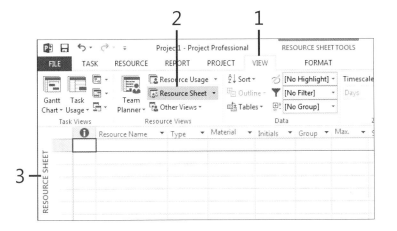

 TIP Shortcuts are available on the Status bar to the Gantt Chart, Task Usage, Team Planner, Resource Sheet, and Report views.

 CAUTION The Team Planner view is available only in Project Professional.

Select a different view (continued)

4 Click the Gantt Chart button to switch the view back to the Gantt Chart view.

5 Note that the view has changed, as shown by the view name.

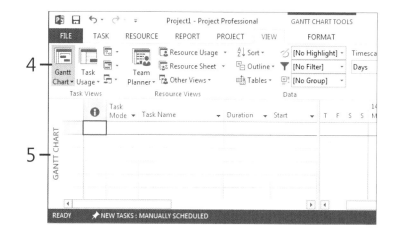

Displaying the View Bar

In addition to the View tab, Microsoft created the View Bar, which displays a graphical list of commonly used views. When enabled, the View Bar is displayed on the left-hand side of the window and provides a quick and easy way to switch between views.

Display the View Bar and choose another view

1 Right-click the view name.

2 Choose View Bar from the menu (it's the last menu item).

3 Click a view within the View Bar to switch to a different view.

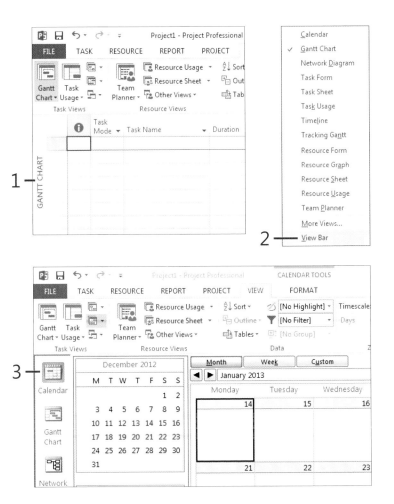

Hide the View Bar

1 Right-click anywhere in the View Bar.

2 Cancel the selection of View Bar from the menu (it's the last menu item).

TIP Displaying and hiding the View Bar is a global setting, so once you have decided to display the View Bar it will appear for all your projects, until you decide to hide it.

TIP The items in the View Bar are displayed alphabetically. If you want to change the display order, you need to change the names of the specific views.

Displaying a different table

Within each view, the table defines the columns that are displayed for each row of information, such as the Task Name, the Resource Name, and so on. It's quite common to switch between different tables in a view—for example, within the

Gantt Chart view you might want to switch to the Tracking Table to update the progress on tasks and then switch back to the entry table to review any changes to scheduled start dates.

Display a different table

1 Check that the view displayed contains a table.

2 Right-click the top leftmost "cell" within the table.

3 Select the desired table from the menu.

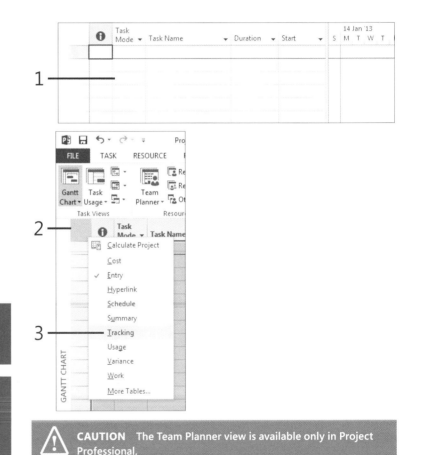

> **✓ TIP** To choose additional tables, click **More Tables** from the menu; when you select a different table, the chart area of the screen does not change.

> **✓ TIP** Not all views contain a table. Built-in views that do not contain a table include the Calendar, Descriptive Network Diagram, Network Diagram, Relationship Diagram, Resource Form, Resource Graph, Resource Name Form, Task Details Form, Task Form, Task Name Form, and Team Planner.

> **⚠ CAUTION** The Team Planner view is available only in Project Professional.

Selecting a different filter

A complex plan might consist of several hundred tasks, sometimes making it difficult to focus on a particular subset of tasks you might be interested in. Project provides a way to filter out the tasks that you don't want to see, leaving just those that

you are interested in. For example, imagine that you are near completion of a project and you want to see only the tasks that haven't been completed. In such an instance you would select and use the Incomplete Tasks filter.

Select the Incomplete Tasks filter

1 Check that the view displayed contains a table.

2 Click the View tab.

3 Click the Filter drop-down list.

4 Select the Incomplete Tasks filter.

> **TRY THIS** Display the AutoFilter (available from the bottom of the filter selection list) to provide a quick way of filtering on different column values within the table area. When the AutoFilter is displayed, a small drop-down arrow is displayed for each column. Click the arrow to select the filter.

> **TRY THIS** Having a quick way to remove any applied filters is very useful. I suggest adding the Clear Filter button to the Quick Access Toolbar or pressing the F3 key to clear the filter.

Selecting a different group

It's possible to group tasks together within the table based on common criteria—for example, you might want to group all the completed tasks together. Grouping of data is most often used to quickly review a set of disparate tasks that have a common criterion.

Select a different group

1 Check that the view displayed contains a table.

(continued on next page)

Select a different group (continued)

2 Click the View tab.

3 Click the Group By drop-down list.

4 Select the desired Group By item.

TIP To select additional groups, choose More Groups from the menu.

TRY THIS Having a quick way to remove any grouping is very useful. I suggest adding the Clear Group button to the Quick Access Toolbar.

Working with and inserting columns in a table

It's often necessary to adjust the default tables within Project. Inserting a column provides a very quick way to check and update specific information (for a task, resource, or assignment) and allows you to update many tasks quickly and efficiently. Other reasons for changing a table might include the following:

- You want to add or hide columns in order to set up a specific view for your customer.

- You have changed the font size of a field, and it no longer fits within the column width. You will need to adjust the width to display the information correctly.

- You have created a custom formula that displays a graphical indicator based on the number of days a task is late.

Project has over 400 predefined columns (and this includes many that can be customized and configured), and at any one time only a fraction can be displayed and viewed within the table area. Inserting (and indeed hiding) columns becomes a necessity depending on what data you need to see at a particular time.

Inserting a column

1 Within the table, click the column to the right of where you want the inserted column to be placed.

2 Click the Format tab.

3 Click the Insert Column button.

(continued on next page)

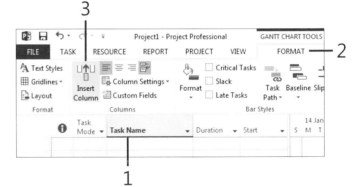

Inserting a column *(continued)*

4 Select the column to insert by typing in the name (if known) or by scrolling through the list.

5 Press Enter.

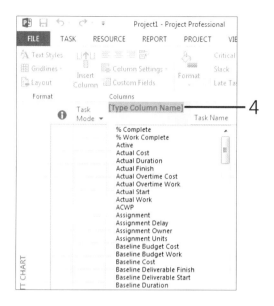

 TIP   If the column width is not correct, move the cursor to the right-hand side of the column boundary until the cursor changes to the Resize Column cursor (✛). Then drag the column left or right to resize it.

 TIP   Typing in the first few letters of the column name will quickly reduce the number of items within the list.

Hiding a column

There is often so much extraneous information in a table that it can be hard to focus on the data that you need to in order to solve a problem or to set up a project schedule correctly. In order to focus correctly, it might be necessary to hide specific columns. Note that in Project a column cannot be deleted or removed, only temporarily hidden.

Hide a column

1 Right-click the column heading that you want to hide.

2 Choose Hide Column from the menu.

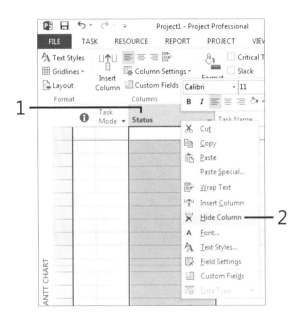

TIP You can quickly hide columns by pressing the Delete key after they have been selected. Please be assured that the data in the column is not removed if you use the Delete key. The Delete key is only a shortcut for hiding the column.

TIP Unlike in Excel, there is no "unhide" a column. To redisplay a column, it must be inserted into the table again.

Moving a column

Columns can be moved left or right and resized. In a table with many columns, moving a column to the left ensures that is it generally visible, especially when you're working on a Gantt chart on a computer with a small screen. There often simply isn't room on the screen to see all of the columns, so moving them around allows the more important ones to be placed where you can see them.

Move a column

1 Left-click the column heading to highlight the column. The Move Cursor icon is displayed.

2 Left-click again on the highlighted column, and drag the column to the desired location (the location is shown using the gray T indicator).

3 Drop the column when it is at the desired location.

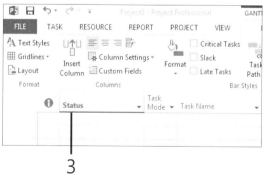

TIP When you move any columns (or indeed rows), the cursor changes from an Arrow icon to the Move Cursor icon (✥). The icon changes to indicate that the column can be moved.

TRY THIS Select the entry table and move the Predecessors column to the left of the task name. This makes manually entering predecessor task numbers much easier when you set up dependencies between tasks.

Resizing a column

Resizing the width of a column often becomes necessary—for instance, when you are inserting a column, the width of the inserted column is set to the same width as the column immediately to the right of it. If your new column displays a simple yes or no value, the new column width is likely to be too large.

Resize a column

1 Move the cursor to the right-hand column border so the cursor changes to a vertical bar with twin arrows (the column resize cursor). Left-click and drag to resize.

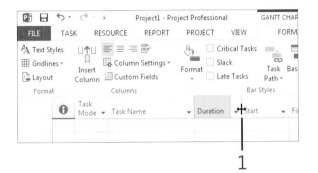

> **TIP** You can autosize columns by double-clicking the column resize cursor. The column will be autosized to the width of the column title, or to the width of the data in the column, whichever is larger. This is a quick and effective way to adjust column sizes.

Saving a modified view

Any modifications that are made to a view will be automatically saved as part of the project. If you want the modifications to be available for all the projects you access, you can save the view with a different name. This automatically saves the table with a new name and the view with the name of your choice.

Save a modified view

1 Click the View tab.

2 Click the drop-down menu from Other Views.

3 Click the Save View option.

4 Type in the name for the view.

5 Click OK.

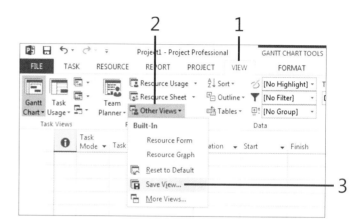

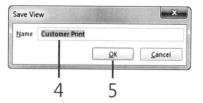

> ✓ TIP Changes you make to any views are automatically saved with the project. However, having spent time crafting a new view, you might want to save it with a specific descriptive name. Make sure the name you choose does not conflict with any other names and that is it meaningful to anyone who might open the project.

Displaying the Project Summary Task

The Project Summary Task displays summary information for the whole project. The Project Summary Task is labeled as Task 0 and summary project information is displayed in the table and chart area.

Display the Project Summary Task

1 In the Format tab, click Project Summary Task.

2 Review the Project Summary Task

Getting the Project basics right

3

The time you spend on "getting the basics right" will be paid back in spades during the project. It's at this stage, at the start of the planning phase of a project, that you are likely to have the time to plan correctly.

Not only is it important to spend some time defining and thinking about your plan, but also it's vitally important that Microsoft Project is set up correctly. Remember that Project is a highly sophisticated tool, designed to help project managers plan, track, and manage projects. As with any sophisticated tool, setting it up correctly to work within the boundaries and constraints that are placed on the project will make using the tool a much easier and more satisfying experience.

When the basic project settings have been defined, the project can be saved; setting the basics won't take too long, and remember, it's time well spent. As well as saving the project to your local storage device, Microsoft allows you to share the project with your colleagues by letting you save it to your SkyDrive, synchronize the tasks to a Microsoft SharePoint 2013 site, or save the plan to a Microsoft Project Server 2013 installation (the latter two options are available only with Project Professional).

In this section:

- Assigning a different calendar as the Project Calendar
- Setting the calendar's working week
- Defining public and organizational holidays
- Defining the calendar options
- Entering the project start date
- Setting the project properties and basic options
- Setting the project currency
- Changing the default view and date format
- Saving the project to a local drive, SkyDrive, SharePoint, or Project Server

Setting up the Project Calendar

A key decision right at the beginning of the project, before any tasks are entered, is to define the standard working hours and working days for the project and the definition of a day. Additionally, some tasks on the project might have to be performed outside of the standard working day, perhaps at night or on a weekend. Of course the majority of projects are run during business hours, but many are run outside core business hours and some run 24 hours a day.

Project installs three basic calendars. It's possible to modify these and create new ones, so regardless of your particular working pattern, you should be in a position to correctly model your organization's working hours. The three basic calendars in Project are named Standard, Night Shift, and 24 Hours.

As you can see from the table, the Project Calendar defines which days per week your organization works and the working times within those days. By default, a new project uses the Standard calendar as the "Project Calendar."

If your project will be run mostly during business hours, you can continue to use the Standard calendar. If your project is run outside of business hours, you will need to change the project calendar to another calendar (Night Shift, 24 Hours, or even a new one). Any calendar may be used as a project calendar, resource calendar, or task calendar. Having selected the calendar, you might need to amend it to match the working periods for your project.

Any additional nonworking times, such as organizational and public holidays, are also held in the project calendar and are defined as Exceptions.

	Standard calendar	Night Shift calendar	24 Hours calendar
Definition	Working time is set as Monday through Friday. Each day starts at 08:00 and finishes at 17:00, with a break between 12:00 and 13:00. This gives a total working time of 8 hours per day, 40 hours per week.	Working time is set as Monday through Sunday. The first shift of the week starts on Monday evening at 23:00 and finishes at 08:00, with a break between 03:00 and 04:00. This gives a total working time of 8 hours per shift, 40 hours per week.	Every day is set as a working day. Each day is set with 24 hours available for working.
Use	When the project will be run during business hours.	When the project will be run overnight.	When the project will run 24/7.

If your organization works eight hours per day, five days per week (Monday to Friday) and cares only that tasks start and finish on a certain day (rather than at a certain time on that day), you do not need to change the Standard calendar.

Assigning a different calendar as the Project Calendar

The Project Calendar defines the default working dates and times within the project. Ensuring that the right calendar is associated with the project is one of the first tasks you need to perform when creating a new project. Microsoft tries to help out and by default assigns the Standard calendar as the Project Calendar.

Assign a different calendar as the Project Calendar

1 In the Project tab, click the Project Information button.

2 Choose the calendar from the drop-down menu.

3 Click OK.

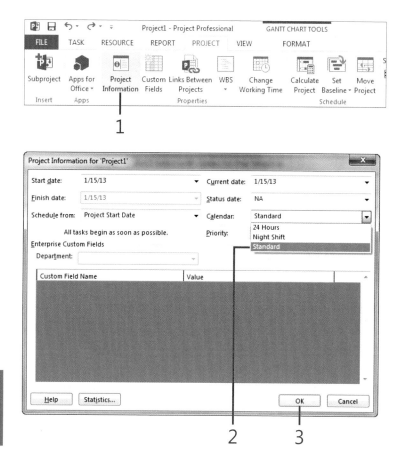

  TIP   Depending on the edition of Project you're using, your screen might look different. For example, the image shows Project Professional. If you're using Project Standard, the dialog box does not display the lower portion of the window.

Setting the calendar's working week

The working week within a calendar defines the working days and the start and finish time for each day. The default Standard calendar is a five-day working week calendar (Monday to Friday), where the working time for each day is defined as 08:00–12:00 and then 13:00–17:00. This provides for 8 hours working time each day, and therefore 40 hours per week. If your organization works eight hours per day, five days per week (Monday to Friday) and cares only that tasks start and finish on a certain day (rather than at a certain time on that day) you don't need to change the Standard calendar.

Set the calendar's working week

1   In the Project tab, click the Change Working Time button.

(continued on next page)

1

 CAUTION   If you change the working times in the Project Calendar, make sure you set the schedule options to reflect these changes.

 TIP   Click in the calendar to verify that the working time for any selected day is correct.

Set the calendar's working week *(continued)*

2 Select the calendar to change from the drop-down list.

3 Click the Work Weeks tab to change the [Default] work week.

4 Click the Details button.

5 Select the days to modify.

6 Choose the appropriate option button and enter the correct working time for the chosen days.

7 Click OK.

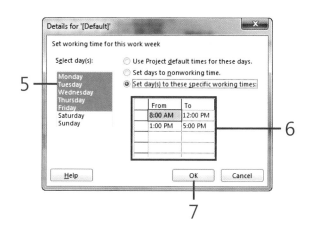

SEE ALSO See "Defining the Calendar Options" on page 44 for more details.

Defining public and organizational holidays

Exceptions to the standard working days, such as public and organizational holidays, should be defined in the Project Calendar. Defining these exceptions ensures that no work is scheduled by default during these holidays, although of course you can override this at a later date if you decide that work does need to occur on a public or organizational holiday.

Define public and organizational holidays

1 In the Project tab, click the Change Working Time button.

(continued on next page)

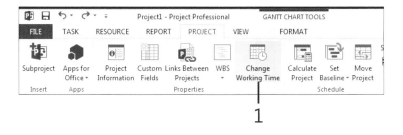

Define public and organizational holidays

(continued)

2 Select the calendar to change from the drop-down list.

3 In the Change Working Time dialog box, click the Exceptions tab.

4 Enter the name, start date, and finish date of the exception.

5 Click OK.

TIP You can make Project enter the exception Start and Finish dates for you. To do this, select the dates in the calendar area and then type in the name of the exception. This is a quick and effective way of entering nonrecurring items such as company holidays.

TIP If the exception occurs regularly, use the Details button in the Exception tab to set the recurrence pattern. The maximum number of reoccurrences for any single exception is 999, and the last recurrence date cannot be beyond 12/31/2149.

Defining the calendar options

In addition to the Project Calendar, Project needs to be told the default start and end times for tasks and how many working hours are in a day and in a week, along with an approximation of how many working days there are in a month.

Project uses the default start and end times and assigns them to tasks when a task start or finish date is entered without a time being specified, and it's important that the default start and end times match the working time as set in the calendar. If the times don't match, you will need to explicitly enter both the date and the time when you enter a task date. By default, Project uses a start time of 08:00 and an end time of 17:00.

Project uses the number of hours in a working day, the number of hours in a working week, and the number of working days per month to calculate data input. For example, if you enter the

duration of a task as two weeks, Project needs to calculate the number of working hours that the two weeks represents and uses the value defined by Hours per week. By default, Project is set up with 8 hours per day, 40 hours per week, and 20 days per month. It's important that the Hours per day and Hours per week values match those defined in the Project Calendar.

Note that if your organization works eight hours per day, five days per week (Monday to Friday) and cares only that tasks start and finish on a certain day (rather than at a certain time on that day), you do not need to change any of the default values. If you are scheduling start or finish times for tasks or you do not work eight hours per day, you will need to amend the working hours per day and associated values. These values are stored as calendar options for the project.

Define the calendar options for the project

1 On the ribbon, click the File tab to navigate to the Backstage view.

(continued on next page)

> **TIP** Remember, if your standard working day is eight hours and you are not concerned about programming the exact time that a task starts or finishes, you can leave these settings unchanged.

Define the calendar options for the project

(continued)

2 In the Backstage view, choose the Options command.

3 Within the Project Options window, select the Schedule category.

4 Amend the times and hours to match your organization's requirements.

5 Click OK.

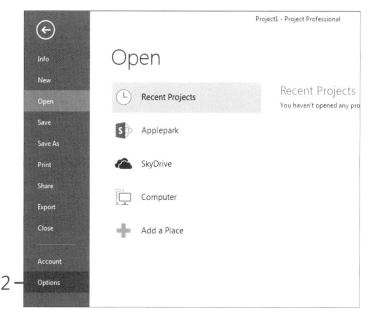

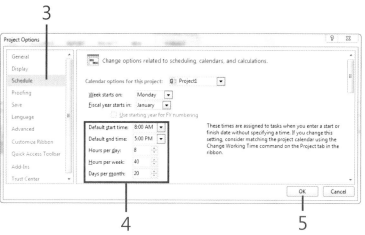

⚠️ **CAUTION** If you change either the Default Start Time, Default End Time, or Hours Per Day values, make sure you change the Project Calendar to match these settings.

🔍 **SEE ALSO** See "Setting the Calendar's Working Week" on page 40 for more details.

Entering the project start date

Entering the project start date might not seem to be the most intuitive place to start, especially when there's an important project to run, right? Wrong. The project start date defines the date on which all new Auto Scheduled tasks start. Setting the project start date also moves the timescale within the Gantt chart and the dates within the Timeline to reflect the start date. It makes little sense to plan to start a project in June and have the timescale displaying dates for April.

Enter the start date

1 In the Project tab, click the Project Information button.

2 Enter the Start date for the project.

3 Click OK.

(continued on next page)

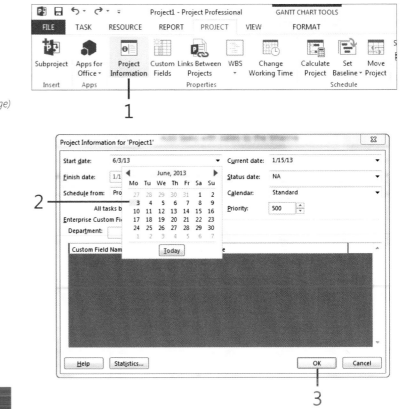

> **TIP** This bottom screen shot is from Project Professional. If you have Project Standard, the dialog box does not have the lower portion of the window.

Enter the start date *(continued)*

4 The timescale with the Gantt chart moves to include the project Start date, and a vertical dotted line is displayed to represent the date.

4

Setting the project properties and basic options

The Project Properties contain items such the project Title, Subject, and Author. It's a great idea to complete these fields because they can be used in headers and footers within reports and they can provide additional information for other users who view the project.

Project contains many options that can affect the look and feel of Project and the way that it performs its scheduling. It's important to note that these options are sometimes set per schedule and some are system-wide.

Set the project properties

1 Click the File tab to access the Backstage view.

2 Choose the Info command.

3 Choose the Project Information drop-down and select Advanced Properties.

(continued on next page)

Set the project properties *(continued)*

4 Click the Summary tab.

5 Enter the project properties as required.

6 Click OK.

4

250G Superior Coffee Properties	?	⊠

| General | Summary | Statistics | Contents | Custom |

Title: 250G Superior Coffee

Subject: New Product Development - 250G Superior Coffee

Author: Ben Howard

Manager: Andrea Cawley

Company: Applepark

Category:

Keywords:

Comments: Produced for PMO

Hyperlink base:

Template:

☐ Save preview picture

[OK]   [Cancel]

5

6

TIP   If you do not edit the Title, Author, and Company fields, the following default values will be used: the Title will be set as the file name when you save the project; the Author will be the user name as defined in the General section of the project options; and the Company field will contain the value entered as the Organization name when Project was installed.

Setting the project currency

If you plan to use and display costs on your project, it's a good idea to make sure that the correct currency symbol is used when you display the costs. When it's installed, Project doesn't use the currency symbol set in your regional settings, preferring instead to use U.S. Dollars (USD). If you are outside of the United States and don't use USD, you should set the project currency accordingly.

Set the project currency

1 Click the File tab to access the Backstage view.

2 In the Backstage view, choose the Options command.

(continued on next page)

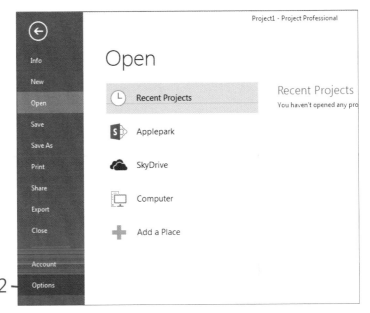

Set the project currency *(continued)*

3 Select the Display category.

4 Enter your currency options for the project.

5 Click OK.

> ⚠ **CAUTION** Project can use only a single currency. If your project has costs in multiple currencies, you will need to convert these and then enter them in Project.

Changing the default view and date format

When you create a new blank project, Project displays the new project using the Gantt With Timeline view because this is set as the default view. If you would prefer a different view as the default, this is the place to change it. In addition to setting the default view, you can also set the preferred date format; the format is influenced by the regional settings of your computer.

Change the default view and date format

1 Click the File tab to access the Backstage view.

2 In the Backstage view, choose the Options command.

3 Click to select the General category.

4 Choose the Default view and Date format from the drop-down lists.

5 Click OK.

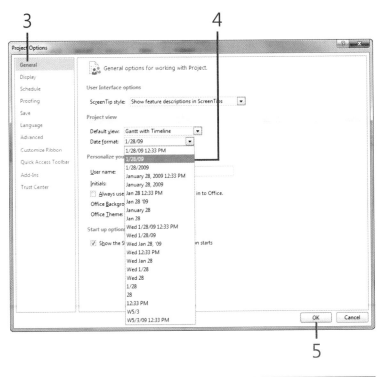

TIP If you choose to display both the date and time (for example, MM-DD-YY HH:MM) or any other date format that is longer than the standard date value, you might need to adjust the width of the Start and Finish date columns in the views to enable Project to display the complete value.

Saving projects

Project allows you to save your file on your hard disk or a network share, on a SharePoint site, to a cloud-based service, or to Project Server 2013. Cloud-based services (such as Microsoft SkyDrive or Microsoft Office 365 SharePoint) store your project in the cloud, allowing you to share the project with colleagues, associates, and friends over the Internet. Project also allows you to save and synchronize the plan with a SharePoint site, which gives team members the ability to interact and update the tasks directly within SharePoint, which can then be synchronized back to the plan. If your organization has installed Project Server 2013 or subscribes to Project Online, Project can save plans directly into your Project Server instance.

When you save a file, it's saved as a project file with the .mpp file type by default. However, you may choose to save the file as a different file type (for example, PDF, Microsoft Excel, and so on). A quick way to save the plan as a different file format is to choose the Export option from the Backstage view.

The first time you save a plan, you will be taken to the Save As command. If you have already saved your plan, Project will save the plan in the same format that was previously chosen. In this section we will save the plan for the first time and review the options we have for the locations for the plan. If you have already saved your plan, to choose another location use the Save As command from the Backstage view.

 TIP Only the Project Professional edition can synchronize plans to SharePoint or save plans into Project Server.

Saving the project to a local drive

A local drive, or indeed a network drive that is mapped as a local drive, is probably the most common location used to save files. When you save a file to a local drive, the file is saved as a Project Plan; however, you can also choose to save the file in other formats, such as Excel or PDF.

Save to a local drive

1 On the Quick Access Toolbar, choose the Save icon.

2 Select Computer.

3 Click Browse to choose the location to save the file to.

(continued on next page)

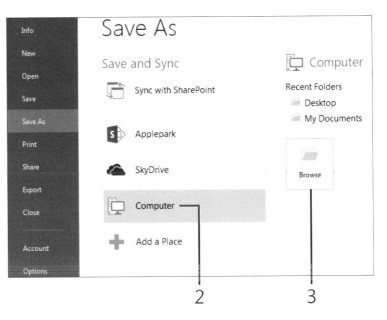

Save to a local drive (continued)

4 Navigate to the location where you want to save the file.

5 Enter the file name.

6 Click Save.

Saving the project to SkyDrive

SkyDrive is a Microsoft service that allows users to save files securely to the Internet and then share those files with friends and colleagues. Not only can you choose with whom to share the file, but you can also choose what access they have to it (read/write, and so on). Saving directly to SkyDrive is built into the Project interface, which makes it very simple to use.

Save to SkyDrive

1 On the Quick Access Toolbar, choose the Save icon.

2 Within the Save As option, choose the appropriate cloud service, and, if prompted, sign in.

3 Within the service, click Browse.

(continued on next page)

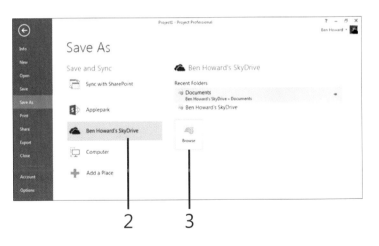

Save to SkyDrive *(continued)*

4 Enter the file name.

5 Click Save.

✓ **TIP** Saving to PDF is a great way to share your plan with other users who don't have a copy of Project. When you save to PDF, the file is created showing the current view—for example, the Gantt Chart view.

✓ **TIP** If you need to share your project with users who have Project 2007 or previous versions, remember to select the right file type or use the Export option from within the Backstage view.

Saving the project to Project Server 2013 or Project Online

Project Server 2013 is a Microsoft product that supports Project Portfolio Management, enabling organizations to manage everyday work across all resources and departments.

Project Server is available either on premise (known as Project Server 2013) or in the cloud as a subscription service (known as Project Online).

Save to Project Server or Project Online

1 Click the File tab on the ribbon.

2 Click the Save As command.

3 Choose the account displayed under Project Web App (mine is called Project Online).

4 Click Save.

(continued on next page)

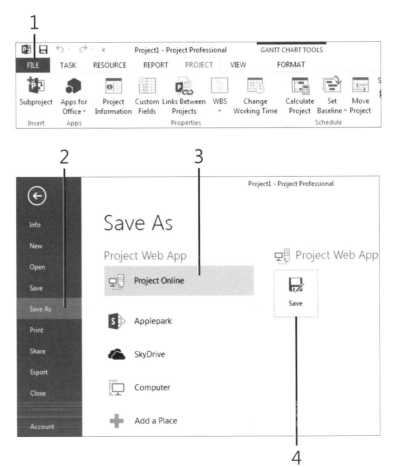

Save to Project Server or Project Online *(continued)*

5 Enter the name of the project.

6 Click Save.

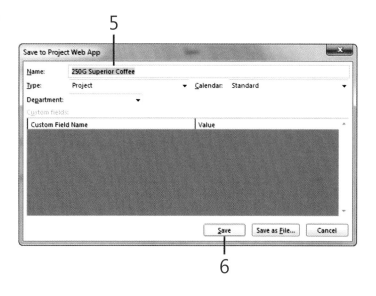

Saving and synchronizing the project to SharePoint 2013

SharePoint is Microsoft's premier collaboration application. Project plans can be saved, and the tasks can be synchronized with a SharePoint site and task list, allowing users who are responsible for completing the tasks to update the status of the task directly in SharePoint. Project Managers can then synchronize the task updates from SharePoint back into the plan. This really is a very smart way to aid the collaboration with the project team.

Save and synchronize with a SharePoint task list

1 On the Quick Access Toolbar, choose the Save icon.

2 Within the Save As option, click Sync with SharePoint.

3 Enter the Project name.

4 Enter the Site address.

5 Click Save.

> **TIP** If you use the Sync with SharePoint option, remember to tell your team members to update their tasks accordingly so that you can synchronize the updates back into your plan.

> **TIP** The Sync with SharePoint option is available only with SharePoint 2013 servers and requires Project Professional 2013.

Creating and modifying tasks

4

A key part of managing any project is defining the tasks that need completing. In project management terms, this list of tasks is called a Work Breakdown Structure, or WBS. Within the WBS, tasks should be grouped together so that the completion of a group of tasks comprises the completion of a significant piece of work. Tasks are grouped together beneath a summary task that will summarize duration, cost, and work totals for a section or deliverable item of work. Each group of tasks should also have a milestone task associated with it. A milestone task is an indicator of a goal date by which the section of work will be completed.

In this section:

- Understanding and setting the schedule mode
- Entering, indenting, and outdenting tasks
- Inserting new tasks into the schedule
- Moving tasks around the schedule
- Moving summary tasks around the schedule
- Deleting tasks

Understanding and setting the schedule mode

To create a project schedule, you enter tasks and create relationships or dependencies between the tasks. The task durations (length of time) along with their relationships to other tasks establish the timeline for a schedule. The schedule mode (also known as the task mode) defines how the scheduling engine in Microsoft Project 2013 will schedule the task. For any individual task the scheduling mode can be either of the following:

- Manually Scheduled
- Auto Scheduled

Manually scheduled tasks

When a task is manually scheduled (this is the default setting), you are in complete control of the task duration, start date, and finish date. During the planning phase of a project, the duration, start date, and finish dates can all be blank or may contain textual information. As task durations, start dates, and finish dates change on predecessor tasks, manually scheduled tasks will not be rescheduled in light of these changes. You can use the Manually Scheduled task mode for preplanning a project, and it gives you the ability to develop a schedule using top-down scheduling (where each significant piece of work, or summary task, is then subdivided into more detailed pieces of work).

Auto scheduled tasks

Tasks that are auto scheduled will always have a duration, start date, and finish date, and because task durations, start dates, and finish dates change on predecessor tasks, auto scheduled

tasks will be rescheduled to reflect these changes. Auto Scheduling mode is the scheduling mode that was used in earlier versions of Project. It allows for bottom-up planning (where the detail tasks are planned and Project accumulates work and cost data into the summary tasks).

You can change the scheduling mode for any task at any time, and the mode is unique per task. Remember that manually scheduled tasks can have incomplete information in the start, finish, or duration values. If the schedule mode of such a task is changed from Manually Scheduled to Auto Scheduled, Project will complete these fields. Both schedule modes may be used within the same project plan.

The following icons are used to visually represent a task's task mode within Project:

Mode	Icon	Comment
Manually Scheduled		Sufficient data is in the Duration, Start, and Finish fields to fully understand when this task will start and finish.
Manually Scheduled		One or more of the Duration, Start, or Finish fields needs additional information in order to know when the task will start and finish.
Automatically Scheduled		The Duration, Start, and Finish fields always contain sufficient data to know when the task will start and finish.

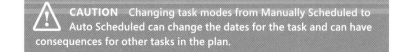

CAUTION Changing task modes from Manually Scheduled to Auto Scheduled can change the dates for the task and can have consequences for other tasks in the plan.

Define the default schedule mode for a project

1 In the Task tab, click the Mode drop-down list.

2 Select the schedule mode for new tasks.

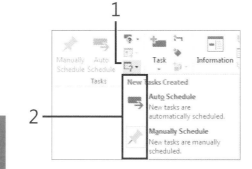

> ✓ **TIP** You can set the default schedule mode for all new projects within the scheduling options. To access the schedule options, click File | Options | Schedule. You will find them in the scheduling options for this project section.

Toggle the task mode for an individual task

1 In the Task tab, click the Gantt Chart button to select the Gantt Chart view. This view contains the Task Mode column.

2 Select the task mode from the drop-down list for the task.

3 Hover the pointer over the Task Mode icon to review the task mode.

4 Click the Task Mode drop-down list to change the task mode back to Manually Scheduled.

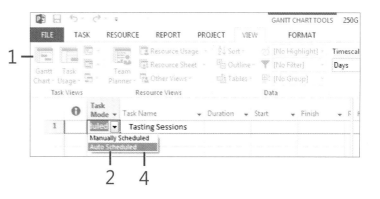

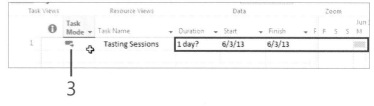

> ✓ **TIP** The schedule mode for new tasks is displayed on the Status Bar and can be changed by clicking the schedule mode on the Status Bar.

Tasks and the Work Breakdown Structure

The set of tasks required to complete a project is known as the Work Breakdown Structure (WBS). The WBS places the tasks in a hierarchy and allows the tasks to be logically grouped together. Logical groups of tasks are called Summary Tasks.

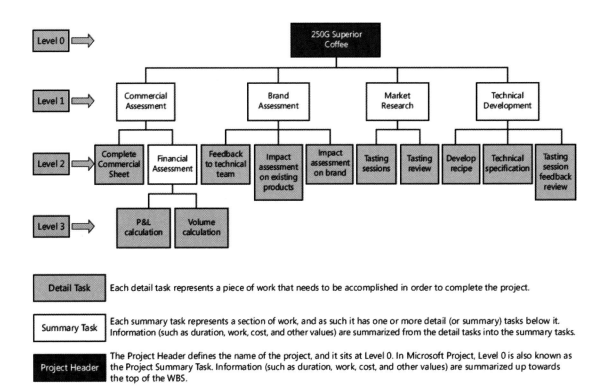

Detail Task — Each detail task represents a piece of work that needs to be accomplished in order to complete the project.

Summary Task — Each summary task represents a section of work, and as such it has one or more detail (or summary) tasks below it. Information (such as duration, work, cost, and other values) are summarized from the detail tasks into the summary tasks.

Project Header — The Project Header defines the name of the project, and it sits at Level 0. In Microsoft Project, Level 0 is also known as the Project Summary Task. Information (such as duration, work, cost, and other values) are summarized up towards the top of the WBS.

Detail, summary, and milestone tasks

Not all tasks are created equal, and Project has three distinct classifications of tasks to help you plan your schedule:

Task classification	Bar Style	Comment
Detail task	Manually Scheduled Auto Scheduled	A detail task (also known as a normal task in Project) represents a discrete piece of work—for example, Complete Commercial Sheet and P&L Breakdown are two detail tasks.
Summary task		A summary task represents a selection or logical grouping of detail tasks—for example, the Commercial Summary task groups together all of the detail tasks that are necessary to fulfil the commercial aspects of the project.
Milestone task		A milestone task is used to define a point in time and does not represent performable work. Milestone tasks are generally used to highlight and report on critical or important events within the schedule.

Entering tasks

Entering tasks correctly is one of the most important actions you will do on your project. The list of tasks (detail tasks) should define the sum of the work required to complete the project. Tasks should be grouped together to provide a hierarchy (called a Work Breakdown Structure, or WBS) for the work using summary tasks, which allows for better organization of the task list. It's best practice for the completion of each grouping of tasks to be represented by a milestone task.

Enter a detail task

1 In the Task tab, click the Gantt Chart button to select the Gantt Chart view (or any task-related view).

2 Click the row header of the task below where you want the new task inserted (this selects the task).

3 Click the Insert Task button.

4 Change the name of the task in the table.

> ✓ **TIP** You can easily enter detail tasks directly into the table area by typing into the Task Name column.

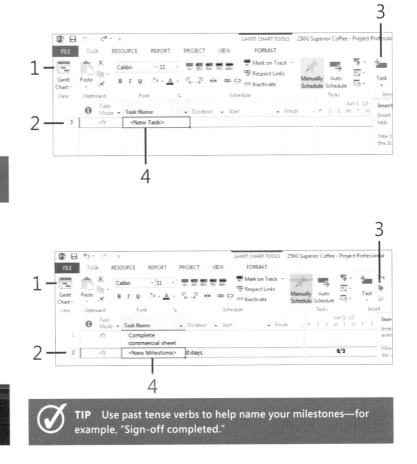

Enter a milestone task

1 In the Task tab, click the Gantt Chart button to select the Gantt Chart view (or any task-related view).

2 Click the row header of the task below where you want the milestone task inserted (this selects the task).

3 Click the Insert Milestone button.

4 Change the name of the milestone task in the table.

> ➔ **TRY THIS** Milestones have zero days duration, so a quick way to create a milestone is to enter a duration of 0 directly in the Duration column in the table.

> ✓ **TIP** Use past tense verbs to help name your milestones—for example, "Sign-off completed."

Enter a summary task

1 In the Task tab, click the Gantt Chart button to select the Gantt Chart view (or any task-related view).

2 Select the tasks that you want to become subtasks of the new summary task.

3 In the Task tab, within the Insert group, click the Insert Summary Task button.

4 Change the name of the new summary task in the table.

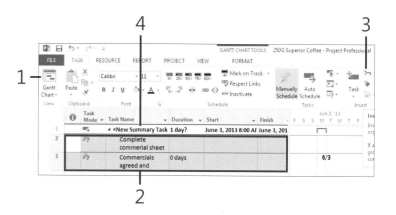

TIP It's easy to visualize the summary tasks because the subtasks within the hierarchy are indented beneath the summary task within the task list.

TIP Summary tasks are always created as Auto Scheduled tasks, and hence their duration will always be equal to the duration of the longest sequence of tasks within their hierarchy. If you want to manually control the number of days duration you require to complete a summary task, change the task mode to Manually Scheduled.

Indenting tasks

When a task is entered into the schedule, it's placed at the same hierarchy level as the task above it. When you build your WBS, you might need to indent a task so that it becomes a subtask of the task above, which becomes a summary task. A task's specific level is called its Outline Level, and tasks can be indented so that their level changes.

Indenting a task has implications for any tasks that become summary tasks as a consequence of the indentation. The specific consequences for the summary task depend upon the task mode and, if the task is manually scheduled, whether a duration value has already been entered for the task. The following table explains the different effects that indenting a task might have for the new summary task:

Task status	Indent effect for the new summary task
Auto Scheduled task	The task becomes a summary task and remains auto scheduled. The start and finish dates are automatically calculated from the earliest start and the latest finish of the subtasks. The duration is automatically calculated as the difference between these two dates.
Manually Scheduled task with no duration	The task becomes a summary task and the task mode changes to auto scheduled. The start and finish dates are automatically calculated from the earliest start and the latest finish of the subtasks. The duration is automatically calculated as the difference between these two dates.
Manually Scheduled task with a duration	The task becomes a summary task and remains manually scheduled. If start and finish dates exist, they are not changed. If they were blank, then they are calculated from the project start date.

Indent a task

1 In the Task tab, click the Gantt Chart button to select the Gantt Chart view (or any task-related view).

2 Click the task row header to select the task that requires indenting.

3 In the Task tab, click the Indent Task button.

4 View the indented detail task and summary task.

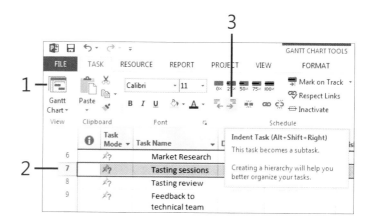

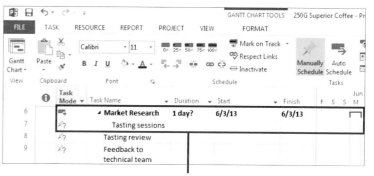

> **TIP** To see the outline level of the tasks, insert the Outline Level column into the table area. The highest level is 0 (representing the Project Summary Task) and the number of levels is virtually unlimited. The more levels that are created, the more complex the WBS might become.

> **TRY THIS** Use the shortcut key of Alt+Shift+Right to quickly indent a task.

Outdenting tasks

When a task is entered into the schedule, it's placed at the same hierarchy level as the task above it. When you build your WBS, you might need to outdent a task so that it sits at the right level. If there are tasks at the same hierarchical level below the task that will be outdented, the outdented task becomes a summary task. A task's specific level is called its outline level, and tasks can be outdented so that their level changes.

Outdent a task

1 In the Task tab, click the Gantt Chart button to select the Gantt Chart view (or any task-related view).

2 Highlight the task that requires outdenting.

3 In the Task tab, click the Outdent Task button.

4 Review the tasks.

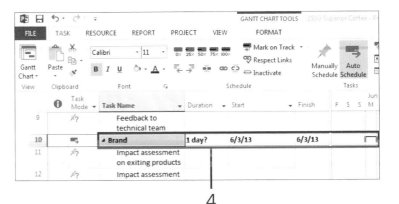

TRY THIS Use the shortcut key of Alt+Shift+Left to quickly outdent a task.

Inserting new tasks into the schedule

Inserting new tasks into the schedule is a very common process, especially during the planning phase, when you are focusing on ensuring that your WBS is complete. Tasks are always inserted at the same outline level as the task above the insertion point. Therefore, you might need to indent or outdent the new task to adjust it to the required outline level.

Insert a task

1 In the Task tab, click the Gantt Chart button to select the Gantt Chart view (or any task-related view).

2 Select the task below where you want the detail task inserted.

3 Click the Task button.

4 Change the name of the task in the table.

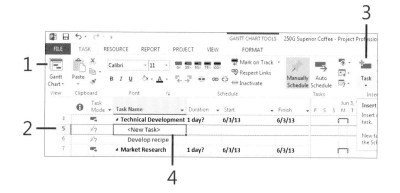

TRY THIS Instead of using the Insert Task button, press the Insert key on your keyboard instead or type directly into a blank row in the sheet.

Moving tasks around the schedule

When you initially create the schedule, tasks (or groups of tasks) might not be displayed in the correct order and might need to be moved up or down the task list. It's possible to move individual tasks, a selection of tasks, or a summary task (which moves all the tasks within its hierarchy). You can move a selection of tasks only if they are next to each other.

When a task is moved within a schedule, its outline level will be changed to equal the outline level of the task that is now immediately above it. Consequently, moving tasks and indenting and outdenting tasks go hand in hand.

Move a single task

1 In the Task tab, click the Gantt Chart button to select the Gantt Chart view (or any task-related view).

2 Select the task by clicking on the task row header.

3 Move the cursor over the task row until the four-arrow cursor (the move cursor) appears.

(continued on next page)

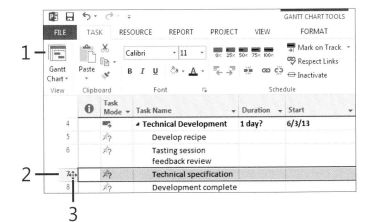

Move a single task *(continued)*

4 Drag the task to the desired location (a horizontal gray line indicates the current cursor position).

5 Review the location of the moved task.

4

	ⓘ	Task Mode ▾	Task Name ▾	Duration ▾	Start ▾	Finish
4		⬛	⊿ Technical Development	1 day?	6/3/13	6/3/1:
5		⚡?	Develop recipe			
6		⚡?	Tasting session feedback review			
7		⚡?	Technical specification			
8		⚡?	Development complete			

	ⓘ	Task Mode ▾	Task Name ▾	Duration ▾	Start ▾	Finish
4		⬛	⊿ Technical Development	1 day?	6/3/13	6/3/1:
5		⚡?	Develop recipe			
6		⚡?	Technical specification			
7		⚡?	Tasting session feedback review			
8		⚡?	Development complete			

5

TIP You can move multiple tasks by left-clicking on the task row header and dragging the mouse up or down to select the desired rows to move. Once the mouse is released, the move cursor appears and you can then click the mouse to drag the rows to the desired location. Only adjacent task rows can be moved together.

Moving summary tasks around the schedule

When you initially create the schedule, tasks (or groups of tasks) might not be displayed in the correct order and might need to be moved up or down the task list. The easiest way to change the order of a group of tasks within the list is to move the summary task, which moves all the tasks within the hierarchy.

When a task is moved within a schedule, its outline level will be changed to equal the outline level of the task that is now immediately above it. Consequently, moving tasks and indenting and outdenting tasks go hand in hand.

Move a summary task

1 In the Task tab, click the Gantt Chart button to select the Gantt Chart view (or any task-related view).

2 Select the summary task by clicking on the task row header.

3 Drag the summary task and all related detail tasks to the desired location (a horizontal gray line indicates the current cursor position).

(continued on next page)

Move a summary task *(continued)*

4 Review the location of the moved summary task (and related subtasks).

5 If the task requires outdenting, click the Outdent Tasks button in the Task tab.

> **TRY THIS** Moving any task places it at the same outline level as the task immediately above it in the entry table. When moving summary tasks, collapse the summary tasks to hide the subtasks and then move the summary task. Not only will this reduce the amount of indenting and outdenting you might need to do, but it will also reduce the number of tasks you see on the screen, allowing you to concentrate on the summary tasks and therefore reduce the amount of scrolling you might need to do.

> **TIP** Cut and paste is also an effective method for relocating tasks. To paste the task(s) at the desired location, click the task below where the tasks are to be inserted and click Paste. There is no need to create available lines before pasting the tasks.

Deleting tasks

During the planning phase, tasks that are no longer required can be deleted.

Delete a task

1 In the Task tab, click the Gantt Chart button to select the Gantt Chart view (or any task-related view).

2 Select the task to delete.

3 Right-click the task row and choose Delete Task from the menu.

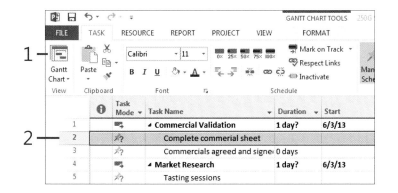

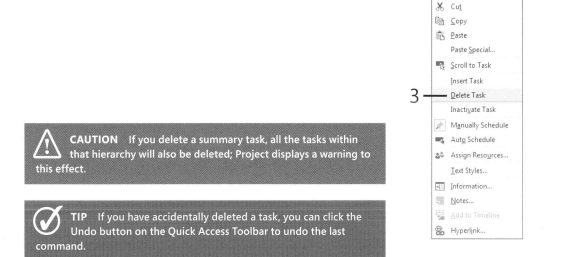

> ⚠ **CAUTION** If you delete a summary task, all the tasks within that hierarchy will also be deleted; Project displays a warning to this effect.

> ✓ **TIP** If you have accidentally deleted a task, you can click the Undo button on the Quick Access Toolbar to undo the last command.

Setting estimates

5

After the tasks are entered in the schedule to create the Work Break-down Structure, the next step is to estimate task durations and work values. Duration is defined as the length of time a task will take to complete. Work is defined as the amount of work (number of hours of effort) it will take to complete the task. For each detail task, you should consider whether it's best to estimate the duration or the work, or both. Estimating these values correctly is not easy and will result in many adjustments until the values are right for the project.

In this section:

- Entering duration estimates for detail tasks
- Entering duration estimates for summary tasks
- Entering work estimates
- Marking tasks that need an estimation review

Entering duration estimates for detail tasks

The duration estimate is an estimate of how long—between the start of a task and the finish of the task—the task will take. Durations are entered by default in days, but they can also be entered in minutes, hours, weeks, or months. If a task is not dependent on the hours worked per day, such as curing concrete, then the duration should be entered as elapsed time; elapsed time is considered waiting time.

For all tasks, Microsoft Project calculates the duration end date for the task based upon the working time as defined in the project calendar. A two-day duration task that starts on a Friday will typically end on the following Monday (because by default Saturday and Sunday are nonworking days).

Enter duration estimates

1   In the Task tab, click the Gantt Chart view.

2   Enter the duration in the Duration column (for example, 2d, which means 2 days).

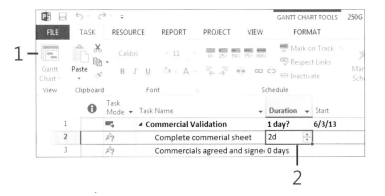

 TIP   When you press Return, the value 2d is converted to 2 days. You may enter values in minutes (m), hours (h), days (d), weeks (w), or months (mo).

TIP   Set a task with a duration of zero days to quickly convert the task to a milestone.

Enter elapsed duration estimates

1 In the Task tab, click the Gantt Chart view.

2 Enter the duration with e in front of the units (for example, 3ed).

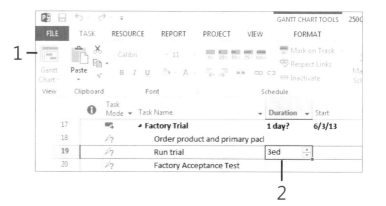

 TIP When you press return, the value 3ed is converted to 3 edays. You may enter elapsed duration values in minutes, hours, days, weeks, or months.

 TIP Elapsed time ignores any nonworking time defined on the calendar.

Entering duration estimates for summary tasks

You can enter duration estimates against summary tasks; doing so will change the summary task into a manually scheduled task if it isn't already. If you are doing top-down planning or have been given a specific duration during which you must complete a phase or a set of tasks, then you might want to enter a duration against a summary task. The duration entered effectively becomes the "duration budget" for the task and by means of the Gantt chart, Project displays whether you are under or over this duration budget. This is a very useful feature when you are decomposing a high-level summary task into multiple detail tasks.

Enter a duration estimate for a summary task

1 In the Task tab, click the Gantt Chart view.

2 Enter the duration against the summary task.

3 Review the change on the Gantt chart.

⚠ CAUTION Entering a duration for a summary task changes it to a manually scheduled task; this might have consequences later if task dependencies have been created between a subtask of this summary task and other auto scheduled tasks.

✓ TIP If you want to remove the duration estimate for a summary task and have the duration calculated from the subtasks, change the task mode for the summary task to auto scheduled.

Entering work estimates

The work estimate is the estimate of the total amount of man days or hours required to complete the task. Entering work estimates is useful when you have a budget in terms of number of days or hours of a resource's time that you have access to or when you have a monetary budget that can then be expressed in a number of days (for example, $5,000 equates to 10 man days at $500 per day).

Entering a work estimate is also useful if you know the task is relatively short but the resource that will perform the task has

a longer period of time to complete it. For example, the work required is half a day (or four hours), but the task will require five days of duration for it to be completed.

Work estimates can be entered only on detail tasks, and the values are rolled up and summarized for each summary task.

Before a work estimate can be entered for a task, the work column needs to be inserted into the table, and once it's inserted it will remain visible until it's hidden.

Enter the work estimates

1 In the Task tab, click the Gantt Chart view.

2 Right-click the Start column title and select Insert Column.

3 Select the Work column from the drop-down list.

4 Enter the work values for the detail tasks.

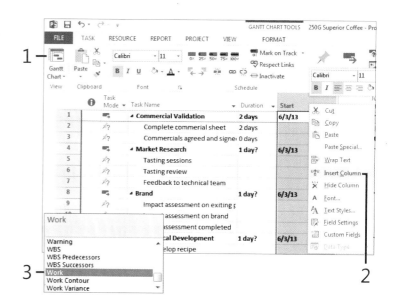

	Task Mode	Task Name	Duration	Work
1	⭤	⊿ **Commercial Validation**	**2 days**	**8 hrs**
2	⚡?	Complete commerial sheet	2 days	8 hrs
3	⚡?	Commercials agreed and signe	0 days	0 hrs

TIP To enter work in hours, just enter the number of hours. You may enter values in minutes (m), hours (h), days (d), weeks (w), or months (mo).

CAUTION Do not enter work for summary or milestone tasks.

Marking tasks that need an estimation review

The process of estimation is often an iterative procedure, so it might take several reviews of an estimate before you feel that it's right for the project. To help with this process, Project allows you to enter durations as estimated by placing a ? after the duration units. For example, 5d? equates to an estimated duration of five days. Both automatically scheduled and manually scheduled tasks can have estimated durations. However,

the estimated flag (denoted by the ? in the Duration field) will be removed for a manually scheduled task when both the start and finish dates are valid and either is modified. Automatically scheduled tasks, once set with an estimated duration, remain as estimated until the task duration is altered, whereupon the ? disappears.

Mark a task with an estimated duration

1 In the Task tab, click the Gantt Chart view.

2 Enter the duration estimate with a ? in the Duration column.

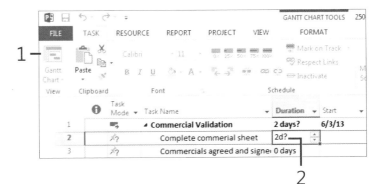

 TIP You can also set the task to be estimated by choosing the Estimated check box in the General tab in the Task Information dialog box. Double-click a task to access the box.

 TIP Automatically scheduled tasks have an estimated duration of one day (1d?) by default.

Linking the tasks

6

Tasks within a project are often dependent upon one another—for example, the completion date of one task determines when another can start. Tasks linked by a dependency are called either a predecessor task (the driving task) or a successor task (the driven task). These links between tasks are called dependencies, and there are four types: Finish to Start, Start to Start, Finish to Finish, and Start to Finish. The default dependency type is Finish to Start.

In this section:

- Linking dependent tasks
- Changing the dependency type
- Unlinking tasks
- Adding a lag or lead time to a dependency
- Displaying task paths

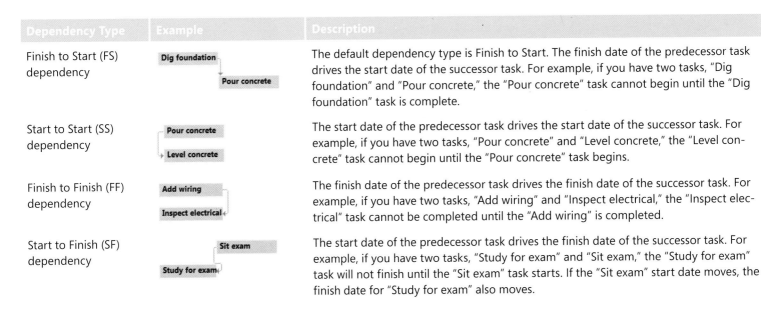

Dependency Type	Example	Description
Finish to Start (FS) dependency	Dig foundation / Pour concrete	The default dependency type is Finish to Start. The finish date of the predecessor task drives the start date of the successor task. For example, if you have two tasks, "Dig foundation" and "Pour concrete," the "Pour concrete" task cannot begin until the "Dig foundation" task is complete.
Start to Start (SS) dependency	Pour concrete / Level concrete	The start date of the predecessor task drives the start date of the successor task. For example, if you have two tasks, "Pour concrete" and "Level concrete," the "Level concrete" task cannot begin until the "Pour concrete" task begins.
Finish to Finish (FF) dependency	Add wiring / Inspect electrical	The finish date of the predecessor task drives the finish date of the successor task. For example, if you have two tasks, "Add wiring" and "Inspect electrical," the "Inspect electrical" task cannot be completed until the "Add wiring" is completed.
Start to Finish (SF) dependency	Sit exam / Study for exam	The start date of the predecessor task drives the finish date of the successor task. For example, if you have two tasks, "Study for exam" and "Sit exam," the "Study for exam" task will not finish until the "Sit exam" task starts. If the "Sit exam" start date moves, the finish date for "Study for exam" also moves.

Each dependency can have a lag time or lead time associated with it. Entering a lag time will delay a task; entering a lead time will cause tasks to overlap.

The effect of linking tasks on schedule data

Linking tasks creates a dependency between the two linked tasks, and Microsoft Project will try to schedule the tasks as a direct consequence of the dependency. Exactly what Project can schedule depends upon the task mode (Auto Scheduled or Manually Scheduled) and the existing data in the Duration, Start, and Finish fields (schedule data).

Linking dependent tasks

Linking tasks together creates a dependency network and starts to show you the order in which the tasks should be completed to successfully manage the project. It's best practice to try and minimize the complexity of links; although, having said that, each nonsummary task in the plan should have both a pre-decessor (except for the task that represents the start of the project) and a successor (except for the task that represents the finish of the project). When you begin to link tasks, try and think about the dependency type because you might need to change it from the default (Finish to Start) to one of the other types.

A single task could have just one predecessor, but in some cases it may have two or more.

Two columns can be used to display the dependency within a table: the Predecessors column and the Successors column. The columns display the Task ID of the relevant Predecessor/Succes-sor. The Task ID is an identifying number that Project automati-cally assigns to each task when it's created, and you can see it in the row header.

In order to create the dependency, you should view the Gantt chart with the entry table because this view contains both the Task ID and the predecessor columns.

The following are all ways to link dependent tasks:

- Drag from one task to another on the Gantt chart or Network Diagram.
- Select tasks to be linked and use the Link The Selected Tasks button in the Task tab.
- Highlight the tasks to be linked and press Ctrl+F2.
- Use the Predecessor tab in the Task Information dialog box.
- Enter the Task ID directly in the Predecessor column or Successor column, or both.

Link dependent tasks

1 In the Task tab, click the Gantt Chart view.

2 Select the predecessor task by choosing the task row header.

3 Select the successor task by Ctrl-clicking the task row header.

4 In the Task tab, click the Link The Selected Tasks button.

5 Review the result of the link in the Predecessors column and the Gantt chart.

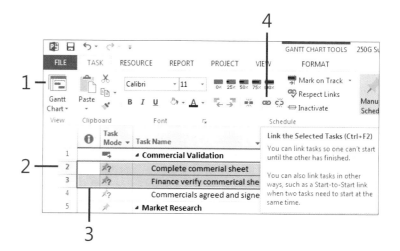

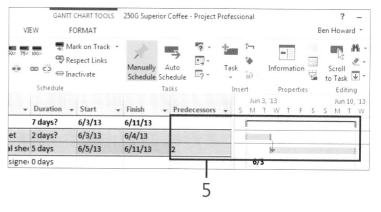

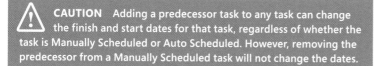

CAUTION Adding a predecessor task to any task can change the finish and start dates for that task, regardless of whether the task is Manually Scheduled or Auto Scheduled. However, removing the predecessor from a Manually Scheduled task will not change the dates.

CAUTION It's best practice not to link summary tasks. Instead, link detail tasks within the summary task and think about creating and linking a milestone to represent the completion of the summary.

Changing the dependency type

The default dependency type is Finish to Start, and although this is the most common dependency used, it's likely that you will need to use the other dependency types, especially when starting one task can lead to the start of one or more other tasks or when the finish of one task can lead to the finish of several other tasks. For example, in a software development project, I can start the testing two weeks after the coding has started. This is known as a Start to Start dependency, and to model it correctly I would add a two-week lag to the testing task (remember that a lag is a period of waiting time).

When a dependency type is not the default (Finish to Start), the dependency type is displayed in the Predecessor and Successor columns, in addition to the Task ID. The dependency type is abbreviated, so a Start to Start dependency is denoted as SS. For example, if the predecessor to a task is Task ID 2 and the dependency type is Start to Start, I would see the value 2SS in the Predecessor column for the task.

The following table summarizes the dependencies and their abbreviations:

Type	Abbreviation
Finish to Start	FS
Finish to Finish	FF
Start to Start	SS
Start to Finish	SF

The following are all ways to change the dependency type:

- Double-click the link in the Gantt chart and change the dependency type.

- Edit the dependency type directly in the Predecessor column or the Successor column, or both.

- Use the Predecessor tab in the Task Information dialog box to change the dependency link.

Change a dependency type using the Predecessor column

1 Click in the Predecessor cell of the task whose dependency you want to modify.

2 Enter the Task ID and the dependency in the cell.

3 Review the result of the link in the Gantt chart.

	Duration	Start	Finish	Predecessors	Jun 3, '13 S M T W T F S	Jun 10, '1 S M T W
	7 days?	6/3/13	6/11/13			
sheet	2 days?	6/3/13	6/4/13			
rical she	5 days	6/5/13	6/11/13	2		
nd signe	0 days				6/3	

1

	Duration	Start	Finish	Predecessors	Jun 3, '13 S M T W T F S	Jun 10, S M T
	7 days?	6/3/13	6/11/13			
et	2 days?	6/3/13	6/4/13			
al she	5 days	6/5/13	6/11/13	2SS		
signe	0 days				6/3	

2

	Duration	Start	Finish	Predecessors	Jun 3, '13 S S M T W T F S
lidation	5 days?	6/3/13	6/7/13		
mmerial sheet	2 days?	6/3/13	6/4/13		
y commerical she	5 days	6/3/13	6/7/13	2SS	
agreed and signe	0 days				6/3

3

> ⚠️ **CAUTION** Changing the dependency type can change the schedule length.

> **TRY THIS** You can also change the dependency type by double-clicking on the dependency link in the Gantt chart. This opens up the Task Dependency dialog box, allowing you to view the associated tasks and change the dependency type.

Changing the dependency type: Change a dependency type using the Predecessor column **89**

Unlinking tasks

As you create and modify your project schedule, chances are you will need to remove existing links and create new ones. You unlink tasks by deleting the links. The following are ways to delete links:

- Double-click the link in the Gantt chart to open the Task Dependency dialog box.

- Edit the Predecessors column, the Successors column, or both.

- Select the tasks to be unlinked and use the Unlink button in the Task tab.

- Use the Predecessor tab in the Task Information dialog box to set the link to None.

Unlink a task using the Task Dependency dialog box

1 In the Task tab, click the Gantt Chart view.

2 Double-click the dependency link in the Gantt chart.

(continued on next page)

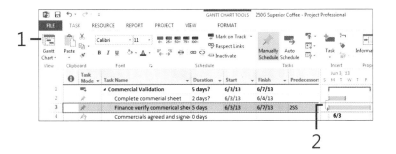

⚠ **CAUTION** Unlinking automatically scheduled tasks changes the start date of the successor task. However, the start date of manually scheduled tasks does not change.

✓ **TIP** To remove all predecessors and successors to a task, select the task and click the Unlink Tasks button (⇥) in the Schedule group in the Task tab.

Unlink a task using the Task Dependency dialog box *(continued)*

3 Click the Delete button.

4 Review the result of deleting the link in the Predecessors column and the Gantt chart.

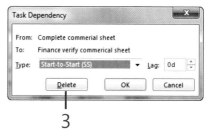

3

	Duration	Start	Finish	Predecessors	Jun 3, '13 S M T W T F S
rcial Validation	5 days?	6/3/13	6/7/13		
plete commerial sheet	2 days?	6/3/13	6/4/13		
ice verify commerical shee	5 days	6/3/13	6/7/13		
nercials agreed and signe	0 days				6/3

4

Adding a lag or lead time to a dependency

In a project, sometimes we need to wait between the end of one task and the start of another. In Project we can enter a number of days to represent this waiting period. This is called a lag. Conversely, we might be able start a task even before its predecessor has finished. Project calls this lead time, and this can also be entered as a number of days. An example of a lag would exist in a construction project, where we might need to wait a week for plaster to dry before it can be painted.

Not only can the lag and lead times be expressed as a duration value (for example, 5 days), but they can also be expressed as a percentage of the predecessor's duration (for example, 50%).

In Project, a lead time is entered as a negative number of days—for example, entering -2 defines a lead time of two days (essentially a lead time is entered as a negative lag time).

The following are ways to add a lag or lead time:

- Double-click the link in the Gantt chart and enter the lag or lead time.

- Edit the lag or lead time directly in the Predecessor column, the Successor column, or both.

- Use the Predecessor tab in the Task Information dialog box to enter the lag or lead time.

Add a lag time by using the Task Information dialog box

1 In the Task tab, click the Gantt Chart view.

2 Select the successor task by choosing the task row header.

3 Click the Task Information button in the Task tab.

(continued on next page)

Add a lag time by using the Task Information dialog box *(continued)*

4 Click the Predecessors tab.

5 Select the predecessor to modify and type in the lag time.

6 Click OK.

7 Review the result of entering the lag time in the Predecessors column and on the Gantt chart.

4

5

Task Information

General | Predecessors | Resources | Advanced | Notes | Custom Fields |

Name: Tasting review   Duration: 2 days ⊕ ☐ Estimated

Predecessors:

ID	Task Name	Type	Lag
6	Tasting sessions	Finish-to-Start (FS)	3d

Help   OK   Cancel

6

	Duration	Start	Finish	Predecessors	Jun 3, '13 S M T W T F S	Jun 10, '13 S M T W T F
	10 days	6/3/13	6/14/13			
	5 days	6/3/13	6/7/13			
	2 days	6/13/13	6/14/13	6FS+3 days		
	1 day	6/3/13	6/3/13			

7

 TRY THIS To create a lag based upon the predecessor's duration, enter a lag time as a percentage (for example, 50%). Then change the duration of the predecessor task and you will see the lag time change for the successor task.

Displaying task paths

Trying to unravel the complexity of a large project plan can be quite difficult, especially with multiple links between tasks and links that might even disappear from the screen. Microsoft has created a new feature called the Task Path that highlights the successors and predecessors in the schedule. The highlighting is displayed in the Gantt chart, and as the user scrolls through the list of tasks, the relevant task paths are highlighted in the Gantt chart, allowing you to see how the selected task fits into the overall schedule. Even more impressive, Project allows you to select multiple tasks, thereby highlighting the task path for several tasks at once.

If a task has multiple predecessors, one or more of those predecessors will directly affect the scheduling of that task; these predecessors are called driving predecessors because they

determine (or drive) when the task starts or finishes. Similarly, when a task has multiple successors, one or more of the successors' start or finish dates will be directly affected (or driven) by the task. These successors are called driven successors because the selected task determines exactly when the successor task is scheduled to occur.

The following items can be highlighted using the Task Path. It's possible to have several items selected at once.

- Predecessors
- Driving predecessors
- Successors
- Driven successors

Display the task path for both predecessors and successors

1 In the Format tab, choose the drop-down menu icon on the Task Path button.

2 Choose Predecessors.

(continued on next page)

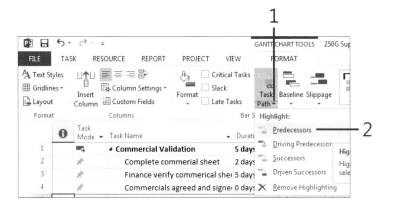

Display the task path for both predecessors and successors *(continued)*

3 Choose the drop-down menu icon on the Task Path button again and choose Successors.

4 Select one or more tasks in the entry table and review the highlighted task paths in the Gantt chart.

TIP Use the cursor keys to move up and down the table to review the predecessors and successors for each task in the Gantt chart.

TIP Add the Driving Predecessors to the Quick Access Toolbar to quickly turn this feature on or off.

Assigning and managing resources

7

Resources are required in order to complete tasks on projects, and once resources are defined, they need to be assigned to tasks. There are three resource types: work, material, and cost. Work resources are used to track work and its related cost, material resources are used to track the materials used and their cost, and cost resources are used to track other independent costs.

When you are adding work resources to a project schedule, it's possible to add them quickly in an ad hoc manner; this can be useful if the resources are assigned to a task full time or if they are used only as an indication of responsibility or ownership of a task. In such an instance, one can assume that the monitoring of workloads or costs is not of significant concern to the project manager. At other times, when workloads and costs are of importance, then resources should be planned carefully and an understanding of the correct use of work, material, and cost resources is required.

Not all projects will require resources on them. Sometimes it's sufficient to just define what needs doing, how long it will take, and in what order tasks need to be completed. If your project falls into this category, you can skip this section.

In this section:

■ Creating work resources quickly in the Gantt Chart view

■ Creating resources using the Resource Sheet

■ Modifying resources

■ Entering resource holidays

■ Assigning work resources to a task

■ Adjusting the work, duration, and assignment units for a task

■ Assigning material resources to a task

■ Assigning cost resources to a task

■ Resolving overallocations

■ Deleting resources

Creating work resources quickly in the Gantt Chart view

Use this option if you are not concerned about tracking costs or other resource information and your goal is to quickly assign resources to tasks and see these assignments in the Gantt Chart view. You might not be interested in the workload that the resource has. Instead, you are concerned with the responsibility or ownership of the task. When resources are created in this manner, Microsoft Project will assign the project calendar and default standard hourly rate to the resource. Using this method to create resources also creates the assignment between the resource and the task, and therefore, a work value for the task is calculated based on the task duration. Only work resources can be created using this method because the work resource is the default resource type. Once a resource has been entered, the same resource may be assigned to multiple tasks.

Create work resources quickly using the Gantt Chart view

1 In the View tab, click the Gantt Chart view.

2 Drag the vertical splitter bar to the right to reveal the Resource Names column.

3 Type the resource name into the field, thereby both creating the resource and assigning it to the task.

TIP Assigning resources to tasks creates work on the task. By default, a one-day duration task with a resource assigned to it using the method described above will create eight hours of work if the project calendar represents an eight-hour day. To see the work value, insert the Work column into the table.

CAUTION Do not assign resources to summary tasks; doing so causes Project to calculate work values at the summary task level.

Changing a resource's working time

When a resource is created, the resource's calendar is copied from the project calendar. Therefore, the resource's calendar contains the same working and nonworking details as the project's calendar.

If a resource works a different number of hours, or even a different shift pattern from that defined by the project calendar, then the resource's calendar might need to be modified to reflect the resource's working pattern.

Once we understand each resource's working time and have set it accordingly, we need to define how much of the resource's working day can be classified as productive time. Productive time is time that can be spent working solely on a project, and nonproductive time is everything else, such as company meetings, staff training, and so on. Some organizations ignore nonproductive time if it's less than four hours per week, and track only significant portions of nonproductive time, such as holidays or training courses. Other organizations assume that resources are productive for 80 percent of their working week, so a day is lost per week doing "admin" type tasks.

The amount of productive time that a resource is available is defined by the Max Units value for a resource. If it's sufficient that your work estimates include admin time, such as answering phones and so on, you can leave the Max Units for each resource at 100 percent. If, however, you want to set a resource's productive time to be less than 100 percent, you can set the resource's Max Units to the value you choose.

Whether you use the concept of productive time or not often depends on how accurate your work estimates need to be.

In addition to the Max Units settings you choose, you might also want to enter larger periods of nonworking time for each resource—for example, holidays or training. These periods are entered as calendar exceptions for each resource, and Project uses these calendar exceptions when a resource is assigned to a task. The effect of the exception will depend on the task mode (Auto Scheduled versus Manually Scheduled) and if Auto Scheduled, the task type (fixed units, work, or duration).

Creating resources using the Resource Sheet

The Resource Sheet is a view within Project that allows the user to view, create, and edit resources and resource information. You can access the Resource Sheet view from the View tab or from the Status Bar (it's the fourth icon in the View Shortcuts area).

Ideally, you should create resources on the Resource Sheet before assigning them to tasks. This method is more formal than the ad hoc method of creating resources by typing their names directly into the Resource Names column on the Gantt Chart view, and it allows for additional entry of resource information, such as resource calendars, resource rates, email addresses, and so on. Adding resources through the Resource Sheet implies a higher level of project management formality and competence.

Three types of resources are available in Project:

- Work resources that are resources or pieces of equipment that perform work to accomplish a task

- Material resources that are project consumables, such as paint

- Cost resources, such as travel expenses

Work resources will require at least a resource name, and, optionally, additional information may be entered, such as resource initials, standard rates, department, accounting code, and so on. The default resource type is Work. A work resource is generally thought of as a person (sometimes known as a named resource) or role, but the term can equally apply to equipment that your organization hires or owns. For example, a work resource could be a cement mixer.

Material resources require a resource name and, optionally, a material label such as "each," cost per unit, cost per use value, and accounting code. For example, coffee can be a material resource. Because it is priced per pound, coffee would have a label of "pound" and the cost would be $10.00. To create a material resource, set the type for the resource to "Material."

Cost resources require only a name and the resource type set to "Cost." For example, a cost resource could be airfare.

Create a resource using the Resource Sheet

1 Select the Resource Sheet by clicking the Resource Sheet shortcut in the status bar.

(continued on next page)

Create a resource using the Resource Sheet

(continued)

2 Click the Resource tab.

3 Click the Add Resources button.

4 Select Work, Material, or Cost Resource from the menu.

5 Overtype the <Resource Name> text with the resource name and complete the other details as necessary.

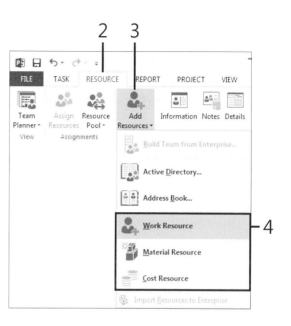

	❶	Resource Name ▼	Type ▼	Material ▼	Initials ▼	Group ▼	Max. ▼	Std. Rate ▼	Ovt. ▼	Cost/Use ▼	Accrue ▼	Base ▼	Code ▼
1		Andrea	Work		A	Accounts	100%	$35.00/hr	$0.00/hr	$0.00	Prorated	Standard	123-654

TIP Adding a standard rate for a material resource allows the cost of the material to be calculated based upon the quantity used. If the standard rate is left at $0.00, the cost of the material will be zero. The value of a cost resource is entered when the assignment is created.

TIP You can easily create work resources that represent an organization, group of people, or role by typing in the representative name—for example, Fabrikam Inc., Finance, or Account Manager. This is useful if you want to identify responsibility for a task away from a named resource to a function or group of people, but it can have implications if you are trying to track the workload and costs associated with that task. This is also known as a generic resource.

Modifying resources

You might need to modify resource details, including the resource's availability, the resource's standard rate, email details, and so on. You can modify resource details by editing the field directly in the Resource Sheet (if the field you want to edit is not available, you will need to insert it), or you can open the Resource Information dialog box to access the fields.

The values that can be modified depend on the type of resource (work, material, or cost). For example, an email address is not applicable for a material resource.

Modify a resource using the Resource Information dialog box

1 Select the Resource Sheet by clicking the Resource Sheet shortcut in the status bar.

2 Click the Resource tab.

3 Select the desired resource by clicking the resource ID in the row header.

4 Click the Information button to open the Resource Information dialog box.

(continued on next page)

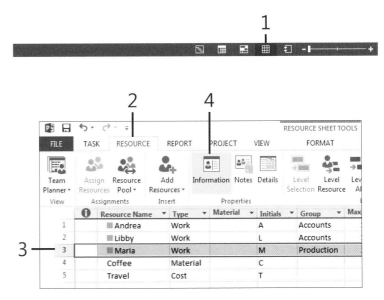

Modify a resource using the Resource Information dialog box *(continued)*

5 Change the desired values and click OK.

TIP You can quickly open the Resource Information dialog box by double-clicking the resource ID or any place in the row for the resource.

TIP Project integrates into Lync, enabling you to see the online status of resources within your contact list. Clicking the Resource Name in the Resource Sheet will display the resource's Lync contact information.

Changing the maximum units for a resource

The amount of productive time that a resource is available is defined by the Max Units value for a resource. If it's sufficient that your work estimates include admin time, such as answering phones and so on, then you can leave the Max Units for each resource at 100 percent. If, however, you want to set a resource's productive time to be less than 100 percent, you can set the resource's Max Units to the value you choose.

Change the Max Units for a resource

1 In the View tab, click Resource Sheet.

2 Change the Max Units for the desired resource.

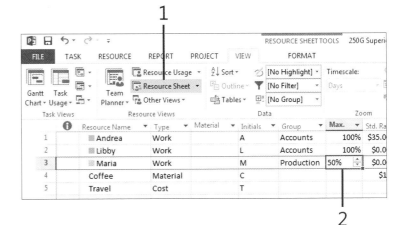

Changing a resource's working day

The amount of time that a resource is potentially available is defined by the resource's working calendar. When a resource is created, that resource inherits a copy of the project calendar (including any exceptions to the standard working week). If the resource works a different number of hours from those defined in the project calendar or a different shift pattern, then you might want to update the resource's calendar to reflect this.

Change a resource's working day

1 In the Project tab, click the Change Working Time button.

2 Choose the resource whose working day you would like to change.

3 Click the Work Weeks tab and highlight the appropriate week.

4 Click the Details button.

5 Edit the specific working times for the work week.

6 Click OK.

7 Click OK to exit the remaining dialog boxes.

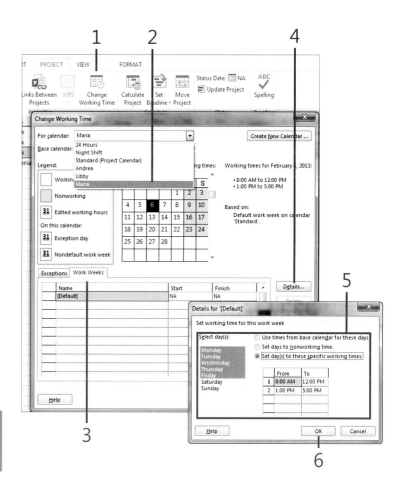

> ⚠️ **CAUTION** Changing the start time for a resource away from the default (8:00 AM) can have scheduling consequences when multiple resources are assigned to the same task.

Entering resource holidays

One of the biggest impacts on a project is resource availability, or, put more correctly, lack of it. It's important that, as a project manager, you track your resource's planned absences so that Project will not schedule the resource to work on vacation.

Enter a resource's holidays

1 In the Project tab, click the Change Working Time button.

2 Choose the Resource whose holiday you wish to enter.

3 Enter the holiday details on a new line in the Exceptions tab.

4 Click OK.

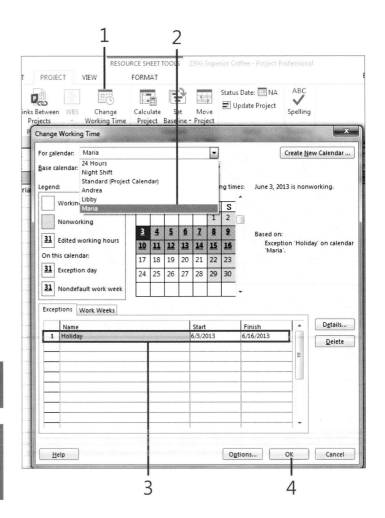

TIP The minimum period you are able to enter for a vacation is a single day.

TIP If the resource is highlighted in the Resource Sheet when the Change Working Time button is selected, the resource will already be selected when the Change Working Time dialog box is displayed.

Setting up a view to assign resources

Much of what we do in Project requires us to be in the right view, at the right time, in order to see the right information. When we assign resources, this is no less important. When assigning resources, I set up my view as follows:

Insert the columns "Type," "Effort Driven," and "Work" into the entry table on the Gantt Chart view.

Check the Details check box in the View tab and select the Task Usage view. Within the Task Usage view, insert the column "Assignment Units."

I am then able to navigate through the task list in the top portion of the screen and view the assignment details for each task in the lower portion of the screen.

You can make changes to Work, Duration, or add or remove resources for a task in the top portion of the screen. When any of these changes are made, Project displays a SmartTag in the top left-hand corner of the cell where you have just made the change. Clicking the SmartTag allows you to review the calculation that Project has chosen and provides you with the option to change Project's decision. Changes to individual assignments, including work or assignment units, can be made in the lower portion of the screen.

Remember that a view can be saved. To do so, click the View tab and select the drop-down menu on the Gantt Chart button. I typically name my saved view "Resource Assignment."

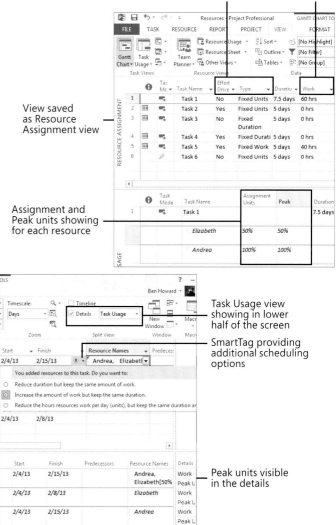

Effort Driven, task Type, and Work columns added

View saved as Resource Assignment view

Assignment and Peak units showing for each resource

Task Usage view showing in lower half of the screen

SmartTag providing additional scheduling options

Peak units visible in the details

How does Project assign work?

Where one or more work resources are assigned to a task, Project uses the following formula for each assignment:

work = assignment units × duration

Work defines the effort, or number of hours, required to complete a task.

Assignment units define what percentage of their working day each resource can devote to a task. The assignment units will initially be set to the Max Units value defined for each resource, but this value can be modified per resource and per assignment.

Duration defines the total number of days between the start and end of a task. By default, duration is displayed in days in Project, where one day is equal to eight hours (this is dependent on the calendar options for the project).

When there is a single resource assigned to a task full time, the formula is very simple. For example, a two-day duration task (which is equivalent to 16 hours) assigned to a resource who works full time on the task will calculate a work value of 16 hours (assuming a calendar of 8 hours per day) (work = 16 hours × 100%).

The scheduling process in Project becomes more complex when either of the following two combinations occurs:

- Resources do not work full time on a project. Instead, their availability is reduced (for example, if they are deemed to be productive for 80 percent of the time, their Max Units would be set to 80 percent, and their initial Assignment Units would also equal 80 percent).

- If, having made an assignment, that assignment is then modified, modifying the assignment could include any of the following:

  - Changing the duration

  - Changing the work

  - Changing the assignment units

  - Adding one or more resources or removing one or more resources from the task

  - Any combination of the above

Let's take a look at the first scenario. If a resource's Max Units is set to 80%, work = duration × 80%, therefore work = 16 × 80% = 12.8 hours, or put another way, working at 80% productivity over two days allows us to accomplish 12.8 hours of work. Again, this is fairly simple to understand.

We can make it a little more complex by modifying either of the work, duration, or (assignment) units. Let's assume we modify the Work value from 12.8 hours to 16 hours, Project has the option to do one of two things. It can increase the units from 80 percent to 100 percent, leaving the duration at 2 days (16 hours); or it can increase the duration from 2 (16 hours) to 2.5 days (20 hours), leaving the units at 80 percent.

Exactly what Project will do depends on several factors. First, if the task is manually scheduled, the duration will not change and the units will increase to 100 percent. If the task is auto scheduled, Project uses a task field called Type to determine which variable to fix and which to change. The three available values for the Type field are Fixed Units, Fixed Work, and Fixed Duration (the default). Project "fixes" the variable defined by the task type and changes the second variable when the third variable is modified. Therefore, for an auto scheduled task with the task type set to the default setting of Fixed Units, increasing the work from 12.8 hours to 16 hours will increase the duration to 2.5 days, leaving the units "fixed" at 80 percent.

Taking the scenario a little further, we might want to add an additional resource to the task. Assuming we have the following task, where there is a single resource completing 16 hours of work in 2.5 days duration, the following options could occur when another resource is added to the task:

- The second resource works at the same rate as the first resource (that is, 80 percent) over the same duration. Hence the work value doubles (duration = 2.5 days, work = 32 hours).

- The second resource works at the same rate as the first resource (that is, 80 percent), but shares the workload of the first resource. Therefore, the work value stays the same (16 hours) but the duration decreases (1.25 days).

- The duration and work values stay the same (2.5 days duration and 16 hours work), but the resources work fewer hours per day, so their units are reduced from 80 percent to 40 percent.

Finally, there is another field, called Effort Driven, that affects auto scheduled tasks. You can set this field to either Yes or No (the default is No). If the task is effort driven (the value is set to Yes), when an additional resource is assigned to the task, the work value for the task is split equally across the resources assigned to the task. Note that fixed work type tasks are deemed to be effort driven by default.

As you can see, getting the correct values set for Work, Units, and Duration for a task involves a little thought and practice. Luckily, Project allows us to set a view that includes all of the fields we need to see in order to successfully manage the variables of Work, Units, and Duration for each assignment.

Assigning a single work resource to a task

Assigning work resources to a task creates work values for the task. The simplest way to assign resources is directly within the Gantt Chart view. This creates a simple assignment where the work value is calculated using the following formula: work = units × duration.

By default, the units for a single resource is 100 percent and, therefore, the work calculated is simply the number of days duration multiplied by the number of hours in a working day (by default, eight hours). I call this the default assignment (where neither the work nor assignment units have been modified).

If you have already created resources by typing their names directly into the Gantt Chart view, then you have already assigned your resources to tasks using the default assignment.

When working with assignments, it's a best practice to have both the duration and work column visible in the entry table, and I have already done this for the remaining screen shots in this section. For information on how to add columns into a table, see Section 2, "Getting started with Project 2013," or Section 3, "Getting the Project basics right."

Assign a single work resource to a task

1 In the View tab, select the Gantt Chart view.

2 Drag the vertical splitter bar (click and hold the bar) to the right to reveal the Resource Names column within the entry table.

(continued on next page)

Assign a single work resource to a task *(continued)*

3 Click in the Resource Names cell for the desired task and select the resource using the drop-down menu.

4 Review the value in the work column to ensure that the calculated value matches your expectations.

	Work	Start	Finish	Predecessors	Resource Names	Jun 3, '13 M T W T F S S
	0 hrs	6/3/13	6/10/13			
	0 hrs	6/3/13	6/4/13			
	0 hrs	6/3/13	6/7/13	2SS		
	0 hrs	6/10/13	6/10/13	3	Andrea	
	0 hrs	6/3/13	6/17/13		Coffee	
	0 hrs	6/3/13	6/7/13		Libby	
	0 hrs	6/13/13	6/14/13	6FS+3 days	Maria	
	0 hrs	6/17/13	6/17/13	7	Travel	

2		Complete commer 2 days	0 hrs	6/3/13	6/4/13	
3		Finance verify con 5 days	40 hrs	6/3/13	6/7/13	2SS
4		Commercials agre 0 days	0 hrs	6/10/13	6/10/13	3

> **TIP** If the Work column is not displayed, you can insert it by clicking the Format tab and then clicking the Insert Column button.

> **TIP** If you are using Lync to communicate with your coworkers and resources, their online status will appear next to their name. To use Lync, enter the email address for the resource in the Resource Information dialog box.

Assigning multiple work resources to a task

Making multiple assignments on one task raises questions of how the work should be spread among the resources—for example, if a five-day duration task has a single assignment, the assignment will total 40 hours of work for the assigned resource (this is the default assignment). If a second resource is then assigned to the task, Project has three options to choose from:

- Spread the existing work between the two resources (resulting in 20 hours of work each), reduce the duration to 2.5 days, leaving the assignment units at 100 percent.

- Spread the existing work between the two resources (resulting in 20 hours work each), reduce the assignment unit for each resource 50 percent, leaving the duration at five days.

- Increase the total work to 80 hours (resulting in 40 hours work each), leave the duration at five days and the assignment units at 100 percent.

The value that changes depends initially upon the task mode (Auto Scheduled versus Manually Scheduled), and if the task is auto scheduled, it will also depend upon the task type (of which there are three: Fixed Units [the default], Fixed Work, or Fixed Duration) and whether the task is effort-driven (definitions of these items are given in the sidebar "How does Project assign work?" on page 108).

Reviewing and setting the task mode, and if applicable, the task type prior to assigning the resources is best practice. With all of these sophisticated components at play, it's recommended to keep a watchful eye on both the duration, work, and assignment unit values for a task while making changes. Luckily, Project makes this easy by providing the ability to insert the Work column in the table and to split the screen horizontally to display more detailed task information. For more information on setting up a view to contain all of these elements, see the sidebar "Setting up a view to assign resources" on page 107.

Remember, Project will use the formula work = units × duration to calculate the amount of work on an assignment. Where there are multiple assignments, the work values for each assignment are rolled up and summarized for the task.

Assign multiple work resources to a task

1 In the View tab, select the Gantt Chart view.

2 Drag the vertical splitter bar to the right to reveal the Resource Names column within the entry table.

(continued on next page)

Assign multiple work resources to a task

(continued)

3 Select the row by clicking the task ID in the row header.

4 Click the Details check box and make sure the task form is displayed.

5 Within the Task Form, right-click the task form (in the lower pane) and select the Work view if it's not already shown.

6 On the task form, select resources from the drop-down list.

7 Click OK.

8 Verify that the work and units values are as you expected, both for the resources and the task.

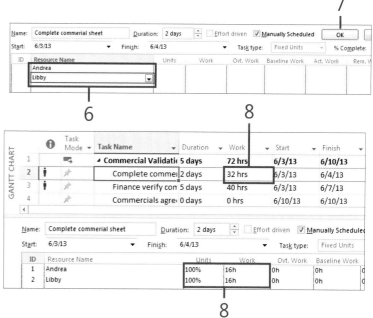

Adjusting the work, duration, and assignment units for a task

When you are assigning multiple resources to a single task, the way that Project distributes the work might not be as you expected or wanted. The best way to make adjustments is to review the data available and then make changes as necessary.

This might be an iterative process so don't necessarily expect to get it right the first time. Remember that Project has an Undo command available on the Quick Access Toolbar, or press Ctrl+Z to undo the last command.

Adjust the work, duration, and assignment units for a task

1 In the View tab, select the Gantt Chart view.

2 Move the vertical splitter bar to the right to reveal the Resource Names column in the entry table.

3 Select the row by clicking the task ID in the row header.

4 Click the Details check box and make sure the task form is displayed.

5 Within the task form, right-click the task form (in the lower pane) and select the Work view if not already shown.

(continued on next page)

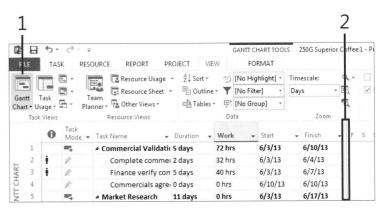

Adjust the work, duration, and assignment units for a task *(continued)*

6 Adjust either the task work or duration fields or the resource work or units fields. If necessary, click OK to update the assignment after the amendments and verify that the work, units, and duration values are as you expect. Repeat as required until the values are correct.

CAUTION The units value displayed in the form is the Assignment units value (this represents the initial assignment units value, which is not necessarily the current one used in the calculation work = units × duration); changing the Work value does not change this (initial) assignment unit value. This is as expected but can cause a lot of confusion.

TIP The impact of the resource assignments and work values on the task is calculated only when the OK button is clicked.

Assigning material resources to a task

When a material resource is assigned to the task, the assignment defines the quantity of the material used and consequently the cost of that material, too. Material resources can't be created on the fly in the same way that work resources can. Material resources always need to be created in the Resource Sheet before they can be assigned to a task. When material resources are assigned, the amount of material required is entered in the Units field. For this example we will use the material resource "coffee," which was previously added to the Resource Sheet; as a reminder, the label for coffee is pound and the price is $10 per pound.

Assign a material resource to a task

1 In the Resource tab, select the Gantt Chart view from the drop-down menu on the Team Planner button.

2 Click the Assign Resources button to display the Assign Resources dialog box.

3 Click the task that you want to make the assignment on.

4 Verify that the selected task name is displayed within the Assign Resource dialog box.

5 Type in the quantity of the required resource in the Units field.

6 Click the Assign button.

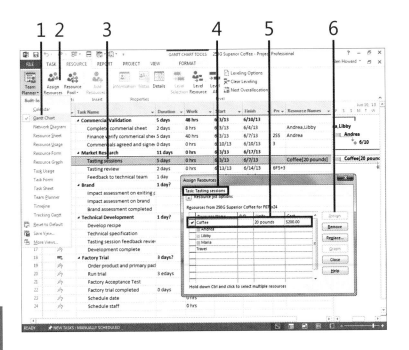

TIP If a standard rate has been entered for the material resource within the Resource Sheet, the cost of the assignment will be displayed.

TIP It's possible to multiselect several tasks and assign the resources to those tasks at once.

Assigning cost resources to a task

Cost resources are typically used to add cost to tasks without adding work hours or task duration. A typical cost that a cost resource would be used for is travel expenses. When the cost resource is assigned to a task, the estimated cost should be entered.

Assign a cost resource to a task

1 In the Resource tab, select the Gantt Chart view from the drop-down menu on the Team Planner button.

2 Click the Assign Resources button to display the Assign Resources dialog box.

3 Click the task that you want to make the assignment on.

4 Verify that the task name is displayed within the Assign Resource dialog box.

5 Type in the estimated cost for the resource on the task.

6 Click the Assign button.

What is an overallocated resource?

Juggling resource demand and availability on a project is another key skill required of the project manager. Project 2013 automatically highlights resources that are overallocated and provides several features to help resolve the overallocations.

When a work resource is assigned to a task, Project calculates the Peak Units value, which reflects the maximum workload that a resource has on an assignment. For example, if a resource is assigned 10 hours of work during a single eight-hour day, the Peak Units field would equal 125%. The Max Units field is defined for each resource on the Resource Sheet and defines the maximum value that the resource is available during the current time period.

An overallocated resource is one where the peak units for any time period exceeds the max units defined for the time period—for example, two tasks running simultaneously with the same resource assigned could give 16 hours of work in an eight-hour day. Tasks with overallocated resources show a "red man" (🔴) in the indicators column in the Gantt Chart view.

There are many ways to view and review overallocations. Any resource that is overallocated is always displayed in red in the Resource Sheet and other resource-centric views. An Overallocated filter is available to quickly identify those resources that are overallocated. In the Team Planner both resources and the conflicting assignments are highlighted in red, and on the Gantt Chart view the "red man" is displayed to indicate tasks where an overallocation exists.

Resolving overallocated resources using the Task Inspector

The Task Inspector button shows both warnings and suggestions for each task. Turning it on displays an additional section of information for each task and is helpful when trying to resolve overallocated resources.

Resolve overallocated resources using the Task Inspector

1 On the Gantt Chart view (or any task-based view), scan the screen for any tasks with the red man icon.

2 Hover over the red man icon and right-click to show the menu options.

3 Select Fix In Task Inspector.

4 Read the specific message regarding the overallocation; the overallocated resources are displayed below the message.

5 Select the appropriate action to resolve the overallocation.

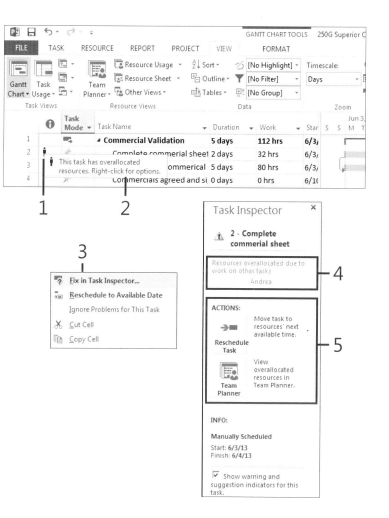

✓ **TIP** You can disable warnings for the task by clearing the Show Warning And Suggestion Indicators For This Task check box.

→ **TRY THIS** Select the Task Inspector from the Task tab by clicking the Task Inspector icon (🔍) in the task group.

Resolving overallocated resources using the Team Planner

The Team Planner view is available in the Professional version of Project, and it allows you to see at a glance which tasks have been assigned to resources. By dragging the tasks between resources you can change existing assignments, remove a resource, from a task, or assign currently unassigned tasks to resources. By dragging the tasks left or right, you can change the dates on which the tasks are scheduled to occur. This is perfectly acceptable for a simple plan, but on a more complex plan with many dependencies and auto scheduled tasks, this can have major scheduling implications. The Team Planner is best suited to viewing and changing assignments between resources rather than rescheduling the start and finish dates of tasks.

Resolve overallocations using the Team Planner

1 In the View tab, select the Team Planner button.

2 Drag the task up or down to change the resource the task is assigned to.

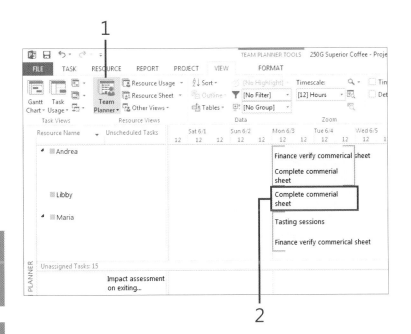

> ⚠ **CAUTION** If the task is auto scheduled, dragging the task left or right will place a constraint date on the task, meaning that the task will be scheduled to start or finish on a specific date. Ideally, each project plan should have a minimal number of constrained tasks.

> ⚠ **CAUTION** If a task is moved outside of the original schedule dates, any dependent tasks will be affected. If the dependent tasks are manually scheduled, they might be marked with a potential scheduling problem in the Gantt chart. If the dependent tasks are auto scheduled, they will be rescheduled automatically and can therefore change the start and end dates on other tasks.

Deleting resources

Sometimes resources are created that are not actually required or used. You should remove these resources from the project because they are not necessary.

Delete a resource

1 In the View tab, click the Resource Sheet button.

2 Click the row heading to select the resource.

3 Press the Delete key to remove the resource.

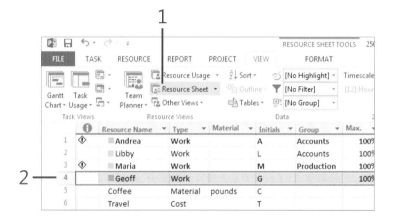

> ⚠ **CAUTION** Deleting a resource also deletes any assignments associated with the resource. If the project has been running for a while, then it's likely that the resource has performed actual work on a project, in which case the actual work will also be removed, causing you to lose historical information regarding the tasks performed by the resource (a warning is shown confirming that you would like to remove the resource). If a resource has left the project, then instead of deleting the resource, it's best practice to reassign the remaining work to another resource and append the word LEFT, followed by the date, to the resource's name. This preserves any actual work or other values that are related to the resource.

Adding external dependencies and deadlines

8

Nobody ever runs a project in isolation. There are simply too many other people who will have some sort of investment, either financial or emotional, in your project. For this reason, company executives, stakeholders, and customers are likely to want to impose deadlines on certain deliverables in the project, and more important, hold you accountable for those deliverables. Understanding and tracking those deadlines is part and parcel of being a project manager.

In addition to the influences you can try and manage (company executives, stakeholders, and customers), there are certain external influences that you can't control, and these will affect your schedule—for example, a product or service you require might not be available until a certain date. There might also be occasions when certain tasks might need to be performed outside of the standard working week, such as on a weekend.

To track deadlines dates for deliverables, Microsoft Project uses the Deadline feature. To specify that a task can't happen until a certain date, Project can "constrain" the task so that it's tied to that date, and if a task needs to be performed outside of the standard project calendar, then it's possible to assign a different calendar to that specific task, allowing Project to schedule the work correctly.

In this section:

- Adding a deadline to a task
- Changing a start or finish date for manually scheduled tasks
- Adding external dependencies for auto scheduled tasks
- Adding a specific calendar to a task
- Planning for tasks that might not happen!

Adding a deadline to a task

A deadline is a target date, created by the project manager, that indicates when a task needs to be completed, rather than when it's scheduled to finish (the finish date). If the task is scheduled to finish after the deadline date, Project displays an icon in the indicator column, telling us that the deadline has passed. The deadline information is entered as part of the Task Information dialog box, and the deadline icon (⬇) is displayed on the Gantt chart.

You can use the following methods to add a deadline date:

- Add the deadline column into the table and directly enter the date.

- Enter the dates in the Task Information dialog box.

Add a deadline to a task using the deadline column

1 In the View tab, click the Gantt Chart button.

2 Right-click one of the column headings.

3 Choose Insert Column from the menu.

(continued on next page)

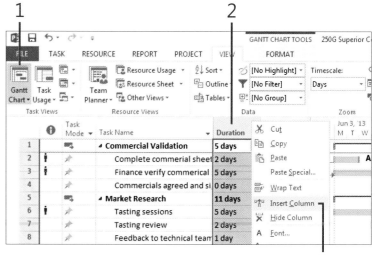

Add a deadline to a task using the deadline column *(continued)*

4 Select the Deadline column from the list.

5 Enter the deadline date for the chosen tasks.

6 Review the deadline indicator on the Gantt chart.

✔ **TIP** If the task finish date is later than the deadline date, a warning indicator (❗) is shown in the indicators column. If you hover over the indicator, a tip appears telling you that the task has gone beyond the deadline edate.

⚠ **CAUTION** Don't use deadlines for all tasks. Choose only the tasks that have a deliverable associated with them. If you enter deadlines for every task, you are collecting too much information on your project and it will soon become unmanageable.

Changing a start or finish date for manually scheduled tasks

Manually scheduled tasks offer a simpler, less complex scheduling experience than auto scheduled tasks, and changing the start or finish dates on a manually scheduled task to reflect an external event will have limited consequences for any linked (dependent) tasks; any linked manually scheduled tasks will not be affected. Linked auto scheduled tasks might be affected, depending on the exact relationship with the manually scheduled task and other tasks.

You can use the following methods to change the dates:

- Enter the dates directly within the table.

- Drag the task bar on the Gantt chart.

- Enter the dates in the Task Information dialog box.

Change the start or finish date for a manually scheduled task

1 In the View tab, click the Gantt Chart button.

2 Enter the desired date for the start date, finish date, or both.

(continued on next page)

TIP Right-click any task where red underlining exists. Project will provide a selection of options to help you correct any potential scheduling problems.

Change the start or finish date for a manually scheduled task *(continued)*

3 Review the changes to the schedule.

	Start	Finish	Pr	3, '13 T W T	Jun 10, '13 S M T W T F S	Jun 17, '13 S M T W T F
s	6/5/13	7/1/1				
	6/5/13	6/18/13				
	6/17/13	6/28/13	26			
	7/1/13	7/1/13	27			

✓ **TIP** Entering start and finish dates for a manually scheduled task will not change the start or finish dates on any linked manually scheduled tasks but might reschedule any linked auto scheduled tasks.

Entering start or finish dates for auto scheduled tasks

Entering start or finish dates for an auto scheduled task will place a constraint on that task. A constraint is a date that can be entered as a Start No Earlier Than, Start No Later Than, Finish No Earlier Than, Finish No Later Than, Must Start On, or Must Finish On constraint type value. The constraint might affect the current schedule and any future schedule changes for that task. Any auto scheduled tasks that are linked to a constrained task might not reschedule when changes are made to task durations because they are date-constrained. Successor manually scheduled tasks will not adjust any date changes to predecessor tasks.

The constraints that are set on a task depend on whether the start or finish date is modified (remember, constraints are set only for auto scheduled tasks).

If the start date is modified, then a Start No Earlier Than (SNET) constraint is set. This moves the task to start on the date specified. It also allows the task to be moved into the future as a consequence of other scheduling changes in the project; however, Project will never schedule the task to start earlier than the specified constraint date.

If the finish date is modified, then a Finish No Earlier Than (FNET) constraint is set. This moves the task to finish on the date specified. It also allows the task to be moved into the future as a consequence of other scheduling changes in the project; however, Project will never schedule the task to finish earlier than the specified date.

In addition to constraining tasks by modifying the start and finish dates, you can add constraints to a task by using the Advanced tab in the Task Information dialog box. This allows the user to choose one of eight constraint types.

Constraints increase the complexity of your schedule and reduce the flexibility of scheduling options. Because of this, use a date constraint only if starting or finishing a task by a specific time is important to the completion of the task or the outcome of the project.

All the constraints except As Soon As Possible and As Late As Possible require a date to be entered into the Constraint Date field. If you manually enter a start date or a finish date, the Constraint Date field is automatically entered for you.

The following table defines the constraint types available in Project:

Constraint name	Description
As Late As Possible	A fully flexible constraint that does not use a constraint date. Project schedules the latest possible start and finish dates for the task, given other scheduling parameters. This is the default constraint type in a project scheduled from the finish date.
As Soon As Possible	A fully flexible constraint that does not use a constraint date. Project schedules the earliest possible start and finish dates for the task, given other scheduling parameters. This is the default constraint type in a project scheduled from the start date.
Finish No Earlier Than	A semi-flexible constraint. The constraint date indicates the earliest possible date that this task can be completed. It can't finish any time before the specified date. For projects scheduled from the start date, this constraint is applied when you type a finish date for a task.
Finish No Later Than	A semi-flexible constraint. The constraint date indicates the latest possible date that this task can be completed. It can be finished on or before the specified date. For projects scheduled from the finish date, this constraint is applied when you type a finish date for a task.
Must Start On	An inflexible constraint. The date indicates the exact date on which a task must begin.
Must Finish On	An inflexible constraint. The date indicates the exact date on which a task must finish.
Start No Earlier Than	A semi-flexible constraint. The constraint date indicates the earliest possible date that this task can begin. It can't start any time before the specified date. For projects scheduled from the start date, this constraint is applied when you type a start data for a task.
Start No Later Than	A semi-flexible constraint. The constraint date indicates the latest possible date that this task can begin. It can start on or before the specified date. For projects scheduled from the finish date, this constraint is applied when you type a start date for a task.

Adding external dependencies for auto scheduled tasks

Auto scheduled tasks offer a very rich scheduling experience, and external dependencies can be represented by entering a constraint type and constraint date against a task.

The consequences of entering a constraint for an auto scheduled task are potentially very great and can change the dynamics of the whole schedule. Before entering constraints, try to understand the effect that it might have on the schedule, and once entered, review any changes made to the schedule. Finally, it's best practice to add a note to each constrained task confirming why the constraint is necessary.

You can use the following methods to enter constraint dates:

- Modify the start or finish dates directly within the entry table (by default, this will create a Start No Earlier Than or Finish No Earlier Than constraint).

- Insert the Constraint Type and Constraint Date columns in the entry table.

- Enter the constraint type and constraint dates in the Task Information dialog box.

- Drag the task bar to the left or right on the Gantt chart.

Add an external dependency for an auto scheduled task

1 In the Task tab, click the Gantt Chart view.

2 Click the task row header for the task that you want to add the constraint to.

3 Click the Information button.

4 Click the Advanced tab in the Task Information dialog box.

5 Select the constraint type.

6 Enter or select the constraint date.

7 Click OK.

8 If a Planning Wizard dialog box appears, choose the option appropriate to your situation.

9 Click OK.

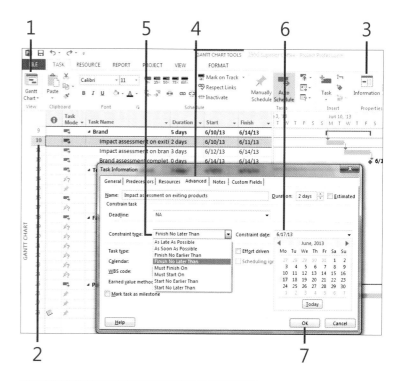

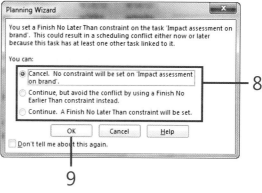

TIP Try to minimize your use of constraints. A project schedule with too many constraints becomes inflexible. Where possible, use deadlines in place of Finish No Later Than constraints. To remove a constraint, set the constraint type to As Soon As Possible in the Advanced tab in the Task Information dialog box.

TIP Constrained tasks have a calendar icon in the Indicators column. Depending on the constraint, it will be either ▦ or ▦.

Adding a specific calendar to a task

There are likely to be occasions when certain tasks need to be completed outside of the normal working day—for example, an office move might happen on a Saturday and Sunday. In such instances you can add a calendar to the task that allows working on Saturday and Sunday. This is known as a task calendar.

Create a new calendar and add a calendar to a task

1 Click the Change Working Time button in the Project tab.

2 Click Create New Calendar.

3 Enter the name of the new calendar.

4 Click OK.

5 Click the Work Weeks tab.

6 Click the Details button.

7 Select Saturday and Sunday and set the days to work specific times.

(continued on next page)

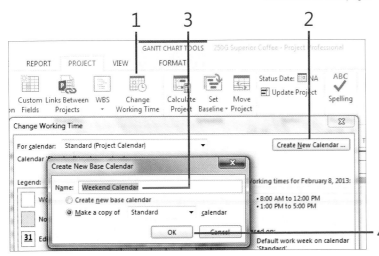

Create a new calendar and add a calendar to a task *(continued)*

8 Multiselect Monday through Friday and set the days to nonworking time.

9 Click OK and then click OK again.

10 Double-click the task row header to display the Task Information dialog box.

11 Click the Advanced tab.

12 Select the calendar to apply to the task.

13 If resources are assigned to the task, select the Scheduling Ignores Resource Calendars check box.

14 Click OK.

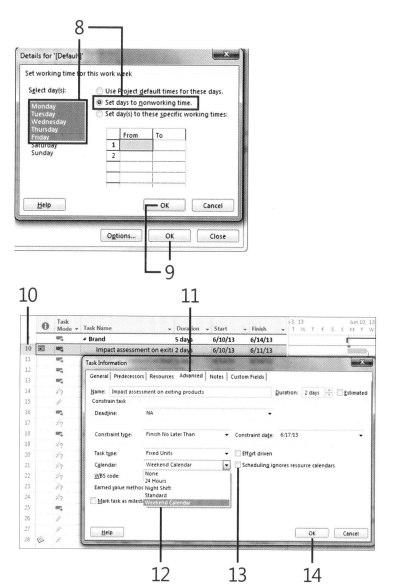

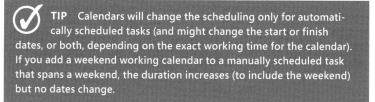

TIP Calendars will change the scheduling only for automatically scheduled tasks (and might change the start or finish dates, or both, depending on the exact working time for the calendar). If you add a weekend working calendar to a manually scheduled task that spans a weekend, the duration increases (to include the weekend) but no dates change.

TIP When you add a calendar to a task, a calendar indicator is added to the indicators column:

Planning for tasks that might not happen!

Sometimes it's not sufficient just to plan for tasks that you know will happen; you might have to plan for tasks that might not happen! There are several reasons why you might want to do this:

- Planning mitigation tasks for risks

- What-if scenarios for planning different options within the project

- Understanding the implications of potential change requests

Project Professional includes a feature called Inactive Tasks.

Making a task inactive or active

1 Click the Task tab.

2 Select the task to inactivate.

3 Click the Inactivate button in the Task tab to inactivate the task.

(continued on next page)

When a task is marked as inactive, the scheduling engine ignores the inactive task. Therefore, inactive tasks might change the scheduling of linked auto scheduled tasks. Inactive tasks remain in the task list and in the Gantt chart but are dimmed to indicate that they no longer affect the schedule.

You can use the following methods to inactivate a task:

- Right-click a task and select Inactivate Task.

- Select the task and click the Inactivate button in the Task tab.

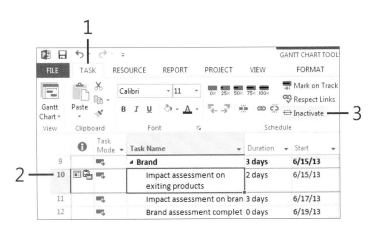

Making a task inactive or active (continued)

4 Review the inactive task and any scheduling changes to other tasks.

5 Click the Inactive button again to activate the task and review the task.

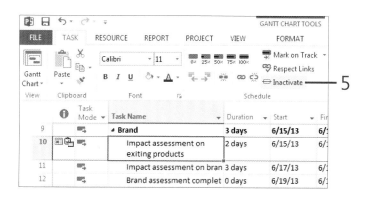

 TIP   Tasks that have already started can't be inactivated.

 TRY THIS   Inactivating a summary task will inactivate all of its subtasks.

Communicating the plan

9

Communication is one of the key project management processes and occurs both informally and formally. Project schedules are typically complex models of real-world scenarios; the ability to quickly simplify and communicate a complex plan to other users is a key project management skill. Microsoft Project provides multiple options for both focusing on specific information and distributing relevant and timely information.

Project contains many options for customizing the look and feel of the Table and Chart areas, including changing font colors, styles, and sizes, changing the color and style of Gantt bars; and changing the text displayed for each Gantt bar. Project also allows you to place custom text and drawing objects on the Chart area.

As in many areas of using Project, the key to successful communication is setting up the view correctly and then deciding whether it should be printed, copied, or emailed! A new feature for this release of Project is the Project Reports; these use a selection of tables, charts, text, and graphical elements to provide a plethora of reporting options. Microsoft has been kind enough to provide over 20 predefined reports; however, if these prove too limiting for you, you can always create your own! Reporting is of such importance that it has its own tab on the ribbon.

Formatting the table area

Project allows you to change the font and color of the text within the table areas to enable specific tasks or types of tasks to stand out. Project already does this by automatically changing the summary tasks to be bold. When formatting tasks, you can format a single cell or a selection of cells (for example, you could change the background cell color to yellow). Or you can change a range of tasks based on an attribute that matches a particular criterion. For example, you could highlight all milestone tasks by setting the font to be italic and blue.

Format a selection of cells

1 Select the cells to format.

2 Click the Task tab, and select the formatting option within the Font group.

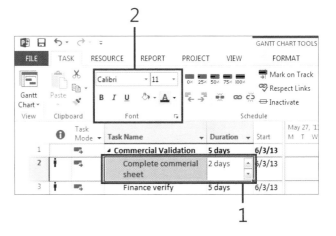

Format all milestone tasks

1 In the Format tab, click the Text Styles button.

2 Choose Milestone Tasks from the Item To Change menu.

3 Select the desired formatting options.

4 Click OK.

5 Review the changes within the table area.

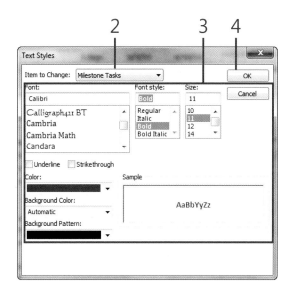

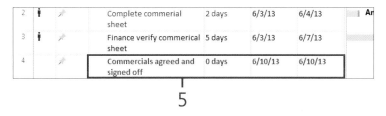

> **TRY THIS** To change tasks that don't match any of the criteria listed, choose Marked Tasks from the Items To Change menu and set the formatting options as desired. Insert the Marked column in the table area and set the tasks you want to change to Yes. Hide the Marked column when you are finished.

Formatting individual bars or a selection of bars

The colors, shapes, and text displayed on the Gantt chart can be changed for individual bars or a selection of bars. This is useful if you want to manually control the format of several bars—for example, you might want to change all of the bars within a phase to be a specific color.

Select and change the format of multiple bars

1. Within the Gantt Chart view, highlight the tasks that you want to change.

2. In the Format tab, click the Format button and choose Bar from the menu.

3. In the Bar Shape tab, use the available options to change the format of the bar shape.

(continued on next page)

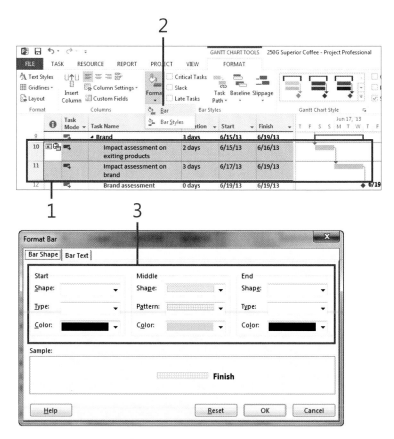

Select and change the format of multiple bars

(continued)

4 In the Bar Text tab, select the text to display for the bars.

5 Click OK.

6 Review the changed bars within the Gantt chart.

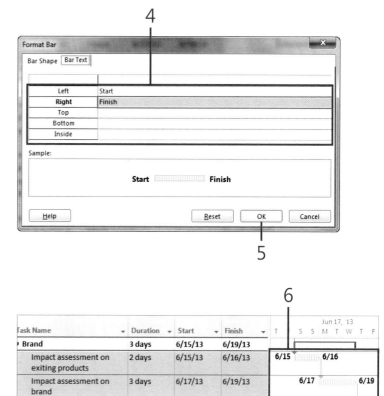

Formatting all the bars at once

Although the Gantt chart is a great way to communicate the project schedule, you might want to change the color scheme for all of the Gantt chart or change the color and text of all the bars that match a certain criterion. Each bar has a specific "Bar Style" that defines the shape, pattern, and color of the bar, plus the text that is displayed next to the bar. Each Bar Style can be unique, but note that if you are using a mixture of auto scheduled and manually scheduled tasks, then you might want to set the text items for both task modes to be the same.

Change the color scheme for all of the Gantt chart

1 Click the Format tab.

2 Select a style from the Style Gallery to apply it.

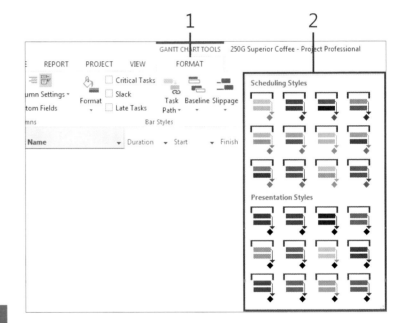

> **TIP** The styles are split into two sections: Scheduling and Presentation. The scheduling styles have different colors for auto scheduled and manually scheduled tasks. The presentation styles use the same color for both task modes.

> **TIP** To return to the default formatting, select the first icon within the scheduling styles gallery.

> **TIP** To change the colors for an individual bar, right-click the specific bar you would like to change and choose the Format Bar menu option. Click the Bar Shape tab in the Format Bar dialog box to change the color only on the selected Gantt bar. Individual settings made in this way will not be overwritten when the bar styles are changed as a whole.

Change the bar styles on the Gantt chart

1 In the Format tab, click the Format button.

2 From the menu, choose Bar Styles.

3 In the Bar Styles dialog box, select the first row, where the row name is Task.

4 In the Bars tab, amend the Shape, Pattern, and Color for the Auto Scheduled Task.

5 Click the Text tab and use the drop-down list to choose which fields to display for each Auto Scheduled) task.

6 Click OK.

7 Review the Gantt chart. The resource's names have been replaced by the Critical field and the Finish field auto scheduled tasks.

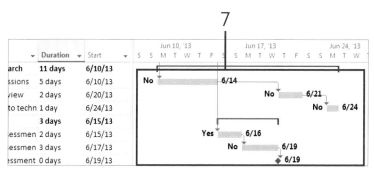

TIP   Manually scheduled and auto scheduled have separate formatting options. Auto scheduled tasks have the name "Task" within the Bar Styles dialog box; manually scheduled tasks are more sensibly named "Manual Task." If you choose to amend a bar style, make sure that you choose the right one (or both!). To change the bar style for all manually scheduled tasks, repeat the above procedure but select Manual Tasks in the Bar Styles dialog box.

Viewing the Task Path

By the time all of the predecessor and successors have been created within a schedule, the Gantt chart can begin to resemble a spider's web! Reviewing the schedule and tracking the paths through the Gantt chart becomes simple thanks to the new Task Path feature, which highlights the chosen Task Path by changing the colors of the bars. A Task Path shows which tasks are influencing the scheduling of predecessor and successor tasks. If you were to print the Gantt chart with the Task Path displayed, the formatting would be preserved for the print.

Display the Task Path

1 In the View tab, select the Gantt Chart view.

2 Select the task whose Task Path you want to highlight.

3 Click the Format tab.

4 Click the Task Path button.

5 Choose Predecessors from the menu.

(continued on next page)

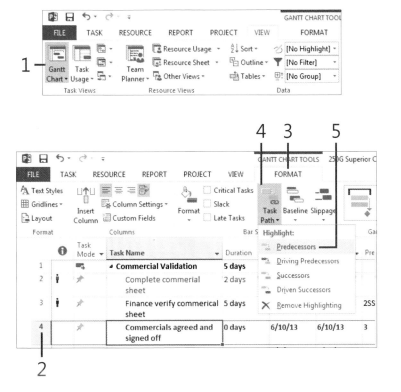

Display the Task Path (continued)

6 Review the formatting change for the task's predecessors in the Gantt chart.

me	Duration	Start	Finish	Pre	Jun 3, 13 S M T W T F S S M T Jun 10
nercial Validation	**5 days**	**6/3/13**	**6/10/13**		
mplete commerial eet	2 days	6/3/13	6/4/13		Andrea,Libby
ance verify commerical eet	5 days	6/3/13	6/7/13	2SS	Andrea,Ma
mmercials agreed and ned off	0 days	6/10/13	6/10/13	3	6/10

TIP You might need to change the timescale on the Gantt chart to review the formatting changes.

TRY THIS Select Driving Predecessors to highlight only the task that immediately drives the selected task.

Displaying the critical path

Executives and stakeholders often want to see the critical path through a project. The critical path is the longest path of tasks through the project based on task duration and relationships. Other scheduling features in Project will also affect calculation of the critical path. If tasks on the critical path are delayed or take longer than originally estimated, the project end date will be affected by the change and the project will be delayed. When you display the critical path, the bars on the Gantt chart for the critical tasks appear in red.

Display the critical path in the Gantt chart

1 Click the Gantt Chart shortcut on the Status Bar to display the Gantt chart.

2 In the Format tab, click the Critical Tasks check box.

3 The color of the bars for the critical tasks on the Gantt chart changes to red.

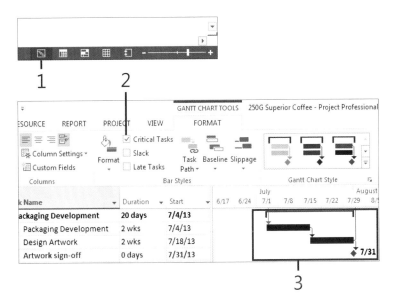

Display only the tasks on the critical path

1 Click the Gantt Chart shortcut to display the Gantt chart.

2 Select the Critical Filter in the View tab.

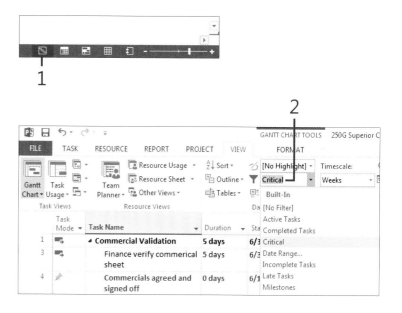

 TIP Press F3 to quickly remove the filter or choose [No Filter] from the Filter menu.

TIP The critical path is the longest path of tasks through the project, based on task duration and relationships, and hence it defines the shortest duration in which the project can be completed. If any task on the critical path slips or moves, it will affect the project as a whole; tasks that are not on the critical path might slip or move without affecting the schedule. The number of days that a task can slip by is called its total slack, and tasks on the critical path have a total slack of zero days. Several scheduling features in Project can affect the critical path calculation, including Deadlines, Constraints, and Elapsed Duration. If you have used any of these features, you might find your critical path is not complete.

Showing and hiding dependency links

When tasks are linked to create a dependency network, the Gantt chart displays the links for each task. When there are many links, the Gantt chart can become very difficult to read.

Turning the dependency links off unclutters the Gantt chart, making it easier to read.

Toggle the dependency links on and off

1 In the Format tab, select the Layout button.

2 In the Layout dialog box, check the option button in the Links section that hides the links.

3 Click OK.

4 Review the Gantt chart.

(continued on next page)

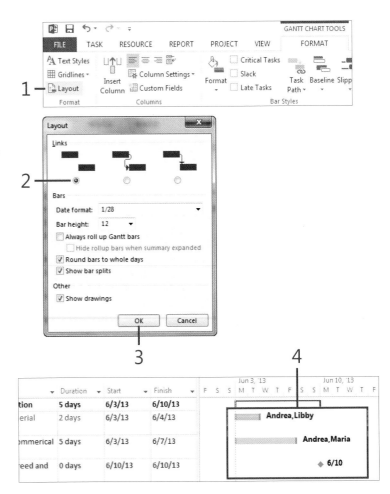

Toggle the dependency links on and off

(continued)

5 To restore the links to the view, reselect the Layout button in the Format tab.

6 Check either of the option buttons in the Layout dialog box that displays the links.

7 Click OK.

8 Review the Gantt chart.

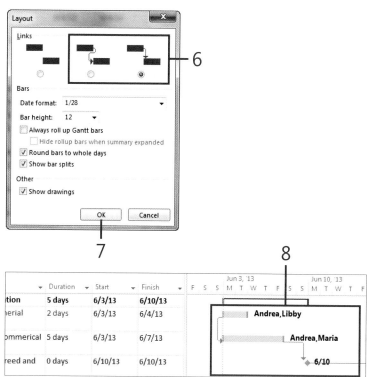

Project 2013 reporting features

The formal reporting within Project 2013 is split into two areas: Project Reports and Visual Reports.

Project Reports are a new feature in Project 2013 and provide a very rich and graphical reporting framework. Project comes preloaded with over 20 predefined reports that use a mixture of tables, charts, images, and text to create the report layout. The data is derived directly from the project schedule. New reports can easily be created and shared with other users, and report themes can easily be modified to change the color scheme. Reports can be printed and copied into other applications. Notable predefined reports include dashboard-style overview reports, resource reports, cost reports, work reports, burndown reports, and in-progress reports.

Visual Reports rely on Microsoft Excel and Microsoft Visio for their generation and presentation and can therefore take advantage of specific features of Excel and Visio. There are many predefined visual reports, based on work, resource, and assignment data. Each predefined report is held as a template, and it's possible to modify these and add new templates. The basis for all reports is cost and work data.

Access to both report types is located in the Report tab.

All reports can either be printed or copied in order to paste them into another application.

A third, less formalized, reporting option is available. As you can print any view within Project, you can meet many reporting requirements by customizing a specific view (often this involves changing the columns displayed in the table, perhaps applying a filter to specify certain tasks, and customizing the look and feel of the Gantt bars) and printing it. This is a very simple and effective way to produce a report that concentrates on a specific area—for example, a milestone report.

Viewing and printing the Project Overview report

Project provides a compelling new reporting feature and comes preinstalled with over 20 reports, nicely categorized for easy access. This new reporting capability allows you to create succinct, vibrant professional reports right in Project, using a combination of charts, tables, graphical images, and much more. All reports are fully customizable, allowing you to modify the existing reports or create new ones to address your organization's specific reporting needs. Once a report has been produced, it can either be printed or copied in order to paste it into another application.

View and print the project overview report

1 Click the Report tab.

2 Click the Dashboards button, and choose Project Overview from the gallery.

3 Review the different components on the report.

(continued on next page)

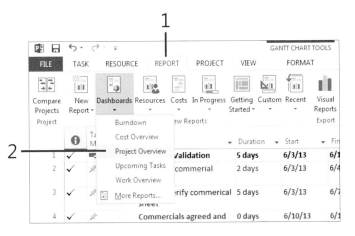

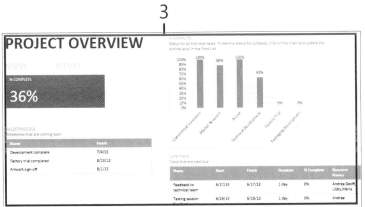

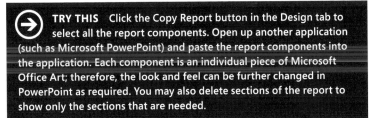

TRY THIS Click the Copy Report button in the Design tab to select all the report components. Open up another application (such as Microsoft PowerPoint) and paste the report components into the application. Each component is an individual piece of Microsoft Office Art; therefore, the look and feel can be further changed in PowerPoint as required. You may also delete sections of the report to show only the sections that are needed.

View and print the project overview report

(continued)

4 Click the File tab.

5 Select the Print option.

6 Select the print options and click the Print button.

4

5   6

Print

250G Superior Coffee - Project Professional   ? — ⊟

Ben Howard

Info

New

Open

Save

Save As

Print

Share

Export

Close

Account

Options

Copies: 1

Print

Printer

Microsoft XPS Document Writer
Ready

Printer Properties

Settings

Print Entire Project
Print the project from start to finish

Dates: 6/3/2013   to 7/1/2013

Pages: 1   to   1

Landscape Orientation

A4
8.27" x 11.69"

Page Setup

PROJECT OVERVIEW

36%

    TIP   To change the color scheme of the report, use the Themes
button in the Design tab.

Viewing and copying burndown reports

Burndown reports are another great new feature of Project 2013. Burndown reports will show graphically how much work has been completed, how much is left to be completed, and how many tasks have been completed and how many are left to be completed.

View and copy the burndown chart

1 Click the Report tab.

2 Click the Dashboards button, and choose Burndown from the drop-down menu.

3 Review the Burndown chart.

(continued on next page)

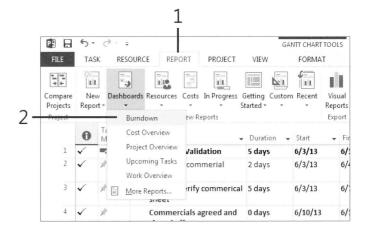

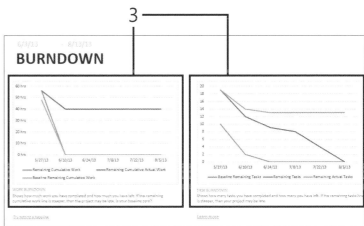

View and copy the burndown chart (continued)

4 In the Design tab, click the Copy Report button.

5 Paste the copied report into Microsoft Word and review it.

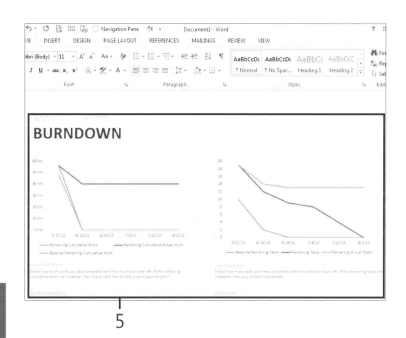

> **TIP** To change the chart style, select the chart and then click the Design tab in the Chart Tools group. Select the desired chart style in the Chart Styles group.

> **TRY THIS** To add your organization's logo to the report, click the Images button in the Design tab. Select the image to place in the report and resize and drag it as desired.

Printing the project schedule

Printing in Project is very similar to printing in other Microsoft Office applications. However, printing only the information that you want to see requires some preparation of the view before you start printing. The ability to review all the pages before they are printed enables you to ensure that your print is exactly as required.

Any view and report can be printed from within Project; the principles discussed in this section can be applied to all views within a plan. For example, you might want to display only the milestones, their summary tasks, and the start and finish dates. Setting up this view requires modifying the table, applying a filter to display only the milestones, and ensuring that all the milestones are visible in the Gantt chart.

Print a milestone report

1 In the View tab, select the Gantt Chart view.

2 Click any column headings you no longer want to see and press the Delete key to hide them.

3 Move the vertical splitter bar left or right so that only the fields you want to print are visible.

(continued on next page)

> **TRY THIS** Add the project title into the header by clicking on the Page Setup, clicking the Header tab, and adding in the project title. Also click the Legend tab and select None to remove the legend from the printed report.

> **TIP** To reset the view back to its original setting, ensure that the view is displayed and then click the Task tab and choose the gallery on the Gantt Chart button. Choose the option Reset To Default.

Print a milestone report *(continued)*

4 In the View tab, select the Milestones filter.

5 Click the Zoom Entire Project button (this ensures that all the milestones are visible on the Gantt chart).

6 Click the File tab.

7 Select the Print option.

8 Choose the print options and click Print to print the milestone report.

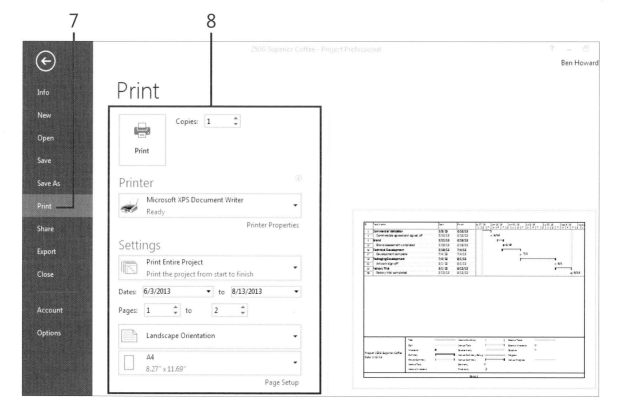

Using Visual Reports

The Visual Reports feature provides additional reporting capabilities by exporting the data from Project into Excel or Visio and then utilizing the powerful number crunching and visualization features of both tools. The source of data for all Visual Reports remains the project plan.

Create a Visual Report in Excel

1 In the Report tab, click the Visual Reports button.

(continued on next page)

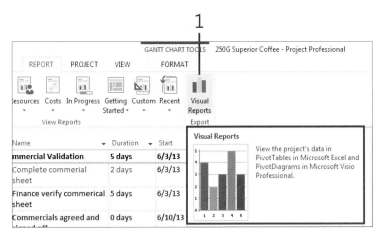

 TIP To use Visual Reports, you need Excel 2010 or Excel 2013 or Visio Professional/Premium 2010 or Visio Professional/Premium 2013.

 TIP Use the Pivot Table fields in Excel or the Pivot Diagram in Visio to select different data fields.

Create a Visual Report in Excel *(continued)*

2 Highlight the report you want to view.

3 Click View.

4 Review the chart in Excel.

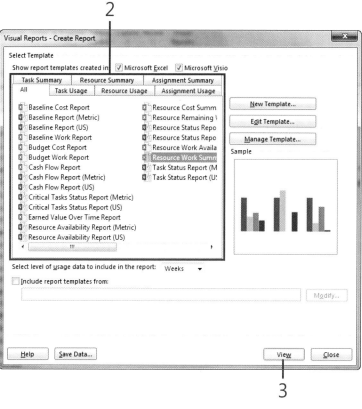

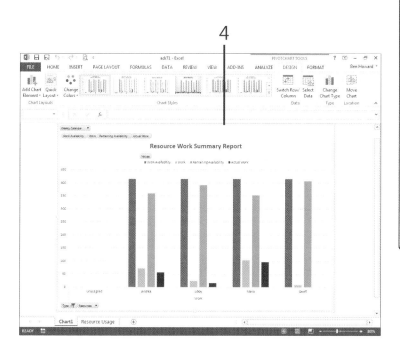

Using the Timeline view

Another favorite view of executives and stakeholders is the Timeline view, which allows you to display key tasks and milestones graphically within a single, concise view. As the project manager, you decide which tasks should be on the Timeline view and how they should be displayed. The Timeline view is automatically updated when the schedule changes, allowing you to concentrate on the best method for communicating the timeline of the project rather than continually updating it.

You can add any task (summary, detail, or milestone) to the timeline. Choose the tasks that best represent the structure and key deliverables of the project, thus providing a succinct overview.

Add a task to the Timeline view

1 In the View tab, select the Timeline check box within the Split View group.

(continued on next page)

1

GANTT CHART TOOLS	250G Superior Coffee - Project Professional

REPORT   PROJECT   VIEW   FORMAT

Resource Usage   ↓ Sort ▾   [No Highlight] ▾   Timescale: 🔍 ▾   ☑ Timeline   Timeline ▾
Resource Sheet ▾   Outline ▾   [No Filter] ▾   Days ▾   ☐ Details
Other Views ▾   Tables ▾   [No Group] ▾

urce Views   Data   Zoom   Split View

> ✓ **TIP** You can quickly add a task to the timeline by right-clicking the task and selecting Add To Timeline.

Add a task to the Timeline view *(continued)*

2 Click in the Timeline View.

3 Click the Format tab.

4 Click the Existing Tasks button.

5 Select the tasks to add to the timeline.

6 Click OK.

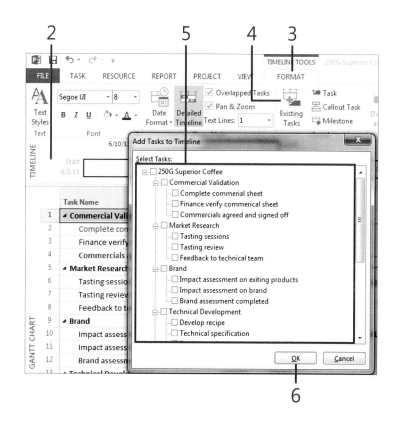

> ⚠️ **CAUTION** Only tasks that have valid start and finish dates can be added to the Timeline. Manually scheduled tasks without start and finish dates cannot be added to the Timeline view.

Formatting the Timeline view

You can format the Timeline view to change the text font, the task format (bar or callout), the date format, and many other features. Format the timeline so that it appears the way you want it to!

Format the Timeline view

1 In the View tab, select the Timeline check box.

2 Click in the Timeline View.

3 Click the Format tab.

4 Highlight the tasks to format on the Timeline view.

5 Select the desired formatting option.

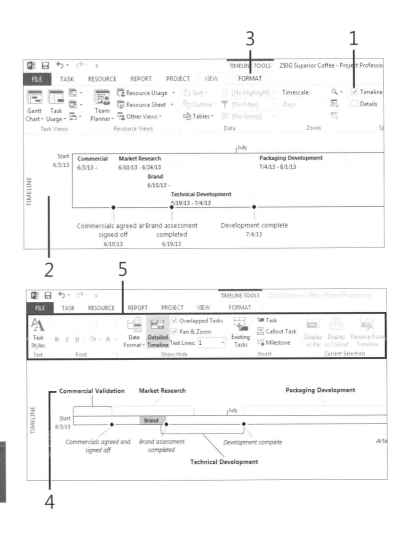

TIP Use the Text Styles button to change the style for specific items—for example, all milestone names could be set to red italics.

Copying the Timeline view to other applications

You can copy the Timeline view to another application, such as PowerPoint, Word, or Microsoft Outlook. The Timeline view is often used as part of a regular status report to provide a concise overview of the project's timescales and key tasks. In the following subtask, we will copy the Timeline view to PowerPoint.

Copy the Timeline view to PowerPoint

1 In the Format tab, click the Copy Timeline button.

2 Choose For Presentation from the menu.

3 Start PowerPoint and paste the Timeline view into your chosen presentation slide.

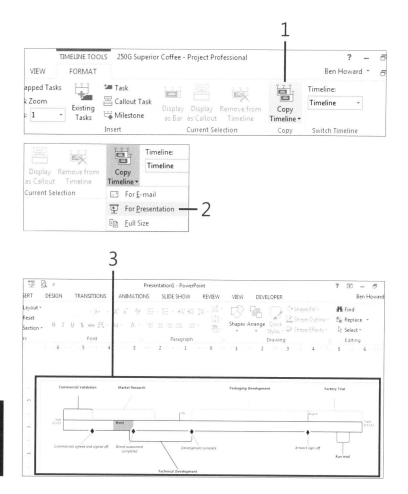

> **TRY THIS**   When you paste the Timeline view, the items are pasted as individual Office Art shapes and therefore you can apply additional formatting, such as reflection and 3-D. This really makes the Timeline view stand out.

Printing the Timeline view

The Timeline view is such a useful view that not only will you want to put it into your PowerPoint presentations, but also you'll want to print it out. In order to print the Timeline view, you will need to view just the Timeline view without other views on the screen.

Print the Timeline view

1 Click the Task tab.

2 Click the down arrow on the bottom of the Gantt Chart button.

3 Select the Timeline view.

(continued on next page)

Print the Timeline view *(continued)*

4 Click the File tab.

5 Choose the Print option.

6 Click the Print button.

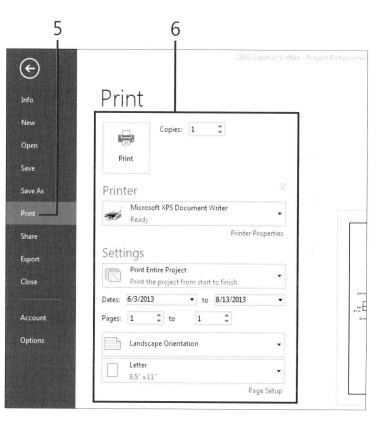

Sharing the plan using SharePoint

There are two primary methods for working with Microsoft SharePoint in Project. The first is to save your Project file to a SharePoint site and the second is to synchronize the tasks in Project with a SharePoint tasks list. This is a very useful method for widely communicating the plan, especially if you also use other SharePoint features, such as document management.

You can save the plan to any version of SharePoint, but the task synchronization will work only on SharePoint 2013. Preconfigured SharePoint sites must be available to receive saved project schedules.

Save a plan to SharePoint

1 Click the File tab.

2 Choose the Save As option.

3 Select the SharePoint icon.

4 Select or browse to a location.

(continued on next page)

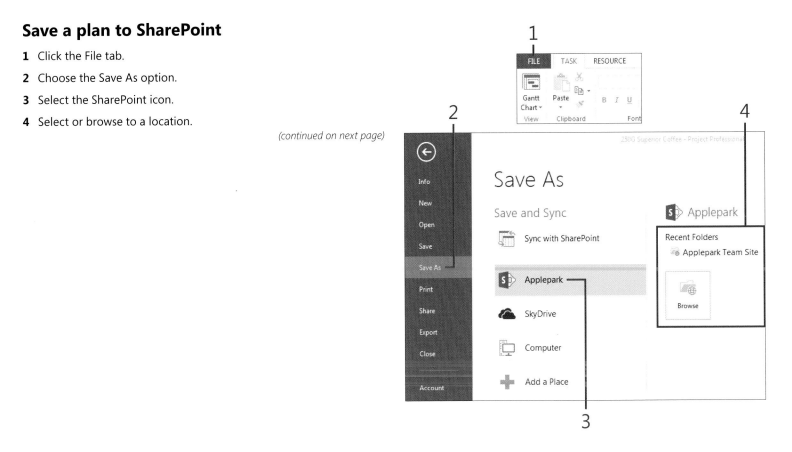

Save a plan to SharePoint (continued)

5 In the Save As dialog box, choose the location.

6 Enter a filename if required.

7 Click Save.

Synchronizing with a SharePoint task list

When a project is synchronized with a SharePoint task list, each project task creates and is linked to the corresponding Share-Point task. Therefore, anyone with access to the SharePoint task list can see the tasks defined on the project. Additionally, team members can update the SharePoint task list, and these updates are applied to the plan when it is next synchronized. You need to have Project Professional to synchronize with a SharePoint task list.

Synchronize with a SharePoint task list

1 Click the File tab.

2 Choose the Save As option.

3 Enter the SharePoint site details to sync with.

4 Click Save.

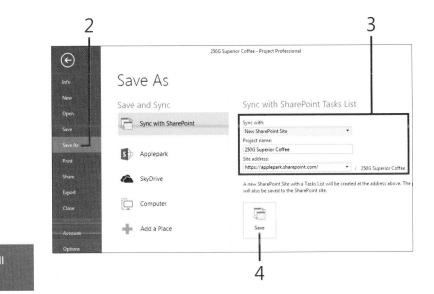

> ✓ **TIP** When you synchronize the task list, the project file will also be saved to the SharePoint site.

Emailing the project schedule

The tool that most of us use more than any other to collaborate with is probably email—some might say it's not so much a collaboration tool as it is a mass communication tool. Regardless of your point of view, it's very handy to be able to email a project schedule to another user.

Email the project schedule

1 Click the File tab.

2 Choose the Share option.

3 Click Email.

4 Click the Send As Attachment button.

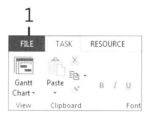

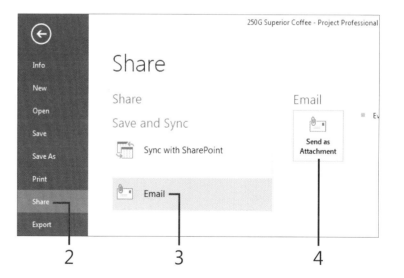

Updating and replanning

10

Taking a baseline, tracking the progress of the tasks, and reviewing the progress against the baseline to understand where and when performance is not going according to plan are part and parcel of the project manager's role. Alas, in many instances, a lack of understanding of how to perform these tasks quickly and efficiently within Microsoft Project means that they are not accomplished, thereby ensuring that the plan quickly becomes outdated.

In this section:

- Setting, clearing, and updating a baseline
- Rescheduling the entire plan to start on a new date
- Updating tasks with %Complete and %Work Complete values
- Setting and displaying the Status Date
- Updating the entire project at once
- Updating Tasks with Actual Values
- Updating Tasks with actual work done per period and remaining work
- Rescheduling uncompleted work to a future date
- Moving tasks forward or backward in the schedule
- Amending remaining duration and work estimates

Setting a baseline

A baseline should be set when all the project tasks and estimates are agreed upon but before any actual work has been recorded on the plan. Ideally, your plan will be signed off by your project sponsor or project board. Baselines are stored for each task, allowing the baseline to be set for single tasks, selected tasks, or more commonly, the entire schedule.

Set a baseline for the entire schedule

1 Click the Project tab.

2 Click the Set Baseline button and choose the Set Baseline option from the menu.

3 Click OK.

(continued on next page)

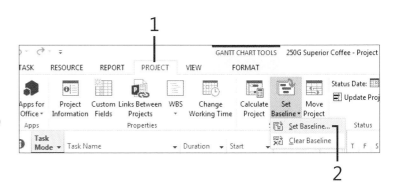

Set a baseline for the entire schedule *(continued)*

4 Click the View tab.

5 Click the Gantt Chart button, and choose Tracking Gantt from the drop-down menu.

6 Review the baseline (the black bars) in the Gantt chart.

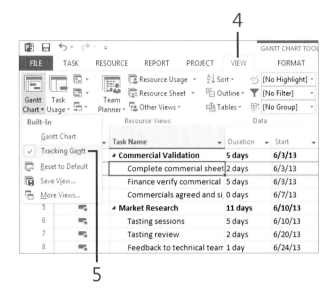

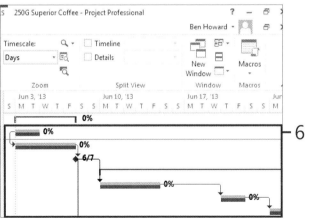

> ✓ **TIP** Along with viewing the Tracking Gantt, change the table to the Baseline table using the Tables | More Tables menu structure from the View tab.

> ✓ **TIP** The date on which the baseline was taken is appended to the baseline name—for example, Baseline (last saved on 2/14/13).

What is a baseline?

A baseline is a snapshot of the schedule at the point in time that you take it, and it includes original schedule information about tasks, resources, and assignments. You can use the baseline to compare what you planned to happen with what actually happened and what is forecast to happen.

Each project can have only a single baseline—that is, the single original state that progress is compared against. When formal changes to the project are agreed upon (and hopefully a consequential agreement to change the project budget, resources, or duration, or all three), the new changes to the schedule can be added into the original baseline; this preserves the baseline for the existing tasks.

In Project, when a baseline is taken, the baseline data is saved into a collection of fields; the duration of each task is saved into a field called Baseline Duration, the start date for each task is saved into a field called Baseline Start, and so on. Project then uses these fields to calculate variances, such as

duration variance, start variance, and so on. These variances show the variance between what was planned (baseline) and the current schedule.

Project includes a specific Gantt chart, called the Tracking Gantt, which uses the baseline fields to display the baseline duration for each task alongside the current duration. Two specific tables, called Baseline and Variance, can be used to review the baseline and variance data within the table area of the screen.

When a baseline is saved, by default it's saved into the collection of fields starting with the name Baseline (Baseline Start, Baseline Finish, Baseline Duration, and so on). There are actually an additional 10 sets of baseline fields (named Baseline1–10) that can also be used to hold data. At any time during the execution of the project, you can use these additional baseline fields for any purpose you want, but primarily they are used for documentation and comparison purposes.

Clearing a baseline

Occasionally it might be necessary to clear a baseline from the plan. The baseline may be cleared for the entire project, a range of selected tasks, or a specific task.

Clear a baseline

1 Click the Project tab.

2 Click the Set Baseline button, and choose Clear Baseline from the menu.

3 Select the baseline to clear.

4 Click OK.

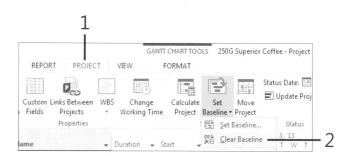

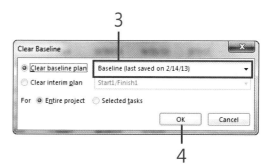

⚠ **CAUTION** Baselines are integral components used when comparing progress on a plan. Be aware of the consequences of deleting a baseline before you do it!

✓ **TIP** If you want to keep a copy of a baseline before you clear it, you can use the Set Interim Plan button in the Set Baseline dialog box to copy values from one baseline set into another.

Updating an existing baseline

Sometimes it's necessary to update an existing baseline. This generally occurs when a formal change request is accepted onto the project and as a result, new tasks are required to be incorporated into the original baseline. The original baseline data will be overwritten by the updated baseline data for tasks that have had a baseline set previously.

Update the baseline

1 Highlight the new task(s) to be added or updated to the baseline.

2 Click the Project tab.

3 Click the Set Baseline button, and choose Set Baseline from the menu.

4 Select the baseline to update.

5 Click the option button for Selected Tasks.

6 Select the check box to roll up baselines to all summary tasks.

7 Click OK.

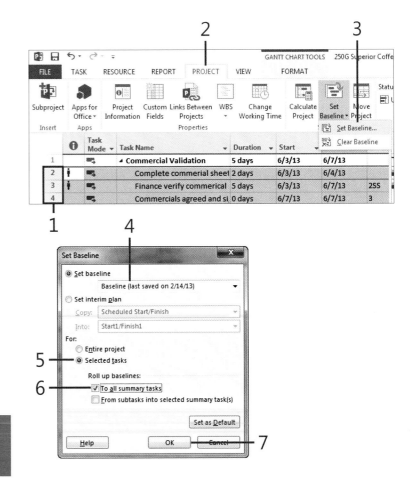

TIP If you want to take a copy of a baseline before you update it, you can use the Set Interim Plan button in the Set Baseline dialog box to copy values from one baseline set into another.

Setting up project views and tables to enable tracking

When updating the project plan, it's advisable to have a view and table selected that provide you with easy access to the relevant columns. When updating tasks using either %Complete, %Work Complete (for a task), or Actual Start and Actual Duration, I recommend using the Tracking Gantt combined with the Tracking table. This combination provides a comprehensive list of fields to update and review.

When updating %Work Complete for resources (when two or more resources are assigned to a single task) or the amount of Work Done Per Period, I use the Task or Resource Usage view.

Understanding the tracking concepts

When a schedule is created, it's originally planned using start fields, finish fields, duration fields, work fields, cost fields, and so on. When a baseline is taken, the entries in these fields are copied into the corresponding set of baseline fields, (Baseline Start, Baseline Finish, Baseline Duration, and so on). When the plan is updated, (which is known as tracking or statusing the plan), actual values will be added to the plan (Actual Start, Actual Work, Actual Cost, and so on), and remaining values are calculated (Remaining Work, Remaining Duration, and so on). Keeping the actual values updated helps you understand what has been done on the project and what remains to be done (for example, Actual Duration and Remaining Duration). Comparing the values against what was planned allows you to see whether you are on track (Baseline Duration versus Duration).

Keeping the plan updated is easy, but it does require some preparation and thought. A key task is to decide what level of detail you need in order to update the plan to your satisfaction, and typically you should select the tracking method based on the type of data you need to manage and report on for project status. You may choose from four main types of update:

- % Complete
- % Work Complete
- Actual Start Date, Actual Duration, and Remaining Duration for a task
- Amount of work done per period and estimated quantity of work required to complete a task

Note that the %Complete field is based on the % Complete of the duration of a task, not the work estimate. If you want to track the percentage of work completed, you should use the %Work Complete field instead.

Only detail and milestone tasks should have their status updated. Summary task values (Actual Start, Actual Duration, and so on) are automatically calculated and updated when their subtasks (detail and milestone) are updated.

Tracking Method	Comments
% Complete	Advantage – Very quick.
	Disadvantage – Doesn't capture an estimate for the remaining work or duration. Usually used when tracking just the schedule and not work on tasks or costs.
% Work Complete	Advantage – Very quick.
	Disadvantage – Doesn't capture an estimate for the remaining work or duration. Usually used when tracking just the schedule and not work on tasks or costs.
Actual Start date, Actual Duration, and Remaining Duration	Advantage – Provides a more accurate view of what has happened and captures an estimate of remaining duration.
	Disadvantage – Requires more keystrokes to update the plan. Team members might not feel comfortable giving estimates to complete, but it provides a more accurate status of a project than % Complete.
Amount of work done per period and estimate to complete	Advantage – Captures the actual work, who did it, and when it was done. Provides an estimate for completion of the task.
	Disadvantage – Each individual assignment requires updating for each time period (usually a day or week). Requires many keystrokes to complete successfully. More work to update the schedule but more complete and accurate information.

Even if you choose to track using %Complete (or %Work Complete), you might still want to capture estimates to complete for these tasks. Choosing one tracking method does preclude you from updating any of the task or assignment values.

Rescheduling the entire plan to start on a new date

Imagine the scenario in which you had planned for a project to start in June only to be told that it was going to be delayed for three months and would now start in September. What you really need is a button that allows you to move all the tasks, along with their constraints and deadlines, forward three months. Luckily, such a button exists! The Move Task button will not only change the start date for the project but also it will reset the deadline and constraint dates accordingly. If you've already taken a baseline, remember to take a new one to reflect the new dates.

Move all the tasks on the plan to a new start date

1 In the Project tab, click the Move Project button.

2 Enter or select the new project start date.

3 Click OK.

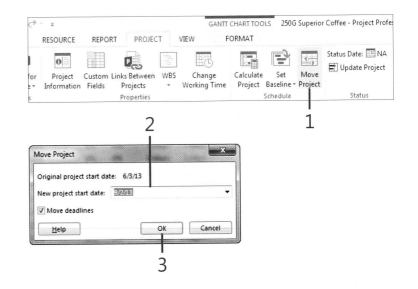

 CAUTION If your project contains tasks with actual values on them, Project will display a warning before moving the tasks.

Should I change the scheduling mode for the tasks?

Many of the examples and screen shots used so far in the book use the default settings, and the default setting for the task mode is Manually Scheduled. When you begin to track a project, the one thing I will guarantee is that what you planned will not happen exactly as you planned it! This is to be expected, and as a consequence, start dates, finish dates, and durations (among many other values) will change. In order to make the updating and replanning of the project as easy and dynamic as possible, consider setting the task mode for the majority (if not all) of your tasks to be auto scheduled. You should do this around the time that you baseline the plan, but definitely before you begin any work on the project. When a task is auto scheduled, its dates will change if the driving predecessor task's dates change, allowing you to quickly assess the impact of the changes to your plan. If you leave all the tasks as manually scheduled, the plan is a static document, and updating it to reflect the new reality is a time-consuming and laborious job.

Updating %Complete for individual tasks

The simplest way to update a project is to update the %Complete field, which represents the percentage of the task's duration that has been completed. This is a very simple but effective tracking measure that will be sufficient for projects where you are tracking only the schedule for a project and where the work completed on a project has a direct relationship with the duration of the task.

Remember to provide status updates only for detail and milestone tasks; the updates to these tasks are rolled up into the Summary Tasks.

Update individual tasks

1 Click the View tab.

2 Select the Tracking table from the drop-down list on the Tables button.

3 Update the %Complete field in the table for the tasks.

(continued on next page)

Update individual tasks *(continued)*

4 Review the changes to the table for the tasks (including Summary Tasks) and the Tracking Gantt.

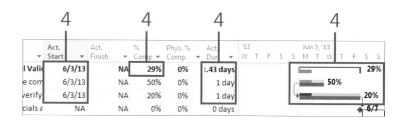

TIP If the %Complete is 25, 50, 75, or 100, you can quickly make the necessary adjustments by using the associated %Complete icons in the Schedule group in the Task tab. If tasks are running as planned, then you can use the Mark On Track button to update the tasks accordingly.

TIP A milestone should either be 0% or 100% complete. Do not set milestones to any other value.

Updating %Work Complete for specific tasks

If you have estimated the amount of work for each task and you track the task status by the work value, then you can use this method to enter the %Work Complete for the tasks. Updating the %Work Complete field will also update the %Complete field. Before you can update the %Work Complete field, you need to insert it into the Tracking table.

Update individual tasks

1 With the Tracking Gantt and Tracking table applied, click the column to the right of where you want the %Work Complete field to be entered.

2 Click the Insert Column button.

3 Choose %Work Complete from the list.

(continued on next page)

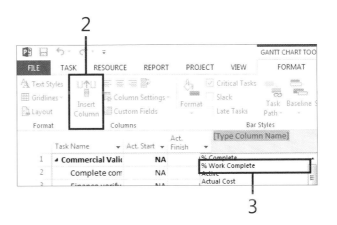

Update individual tasks *(continued)*

4 Update the %Work Complete field in the table for the tasks.

5 Review the changes to the table for the tasks (including Summary Tasks) and the Tracking Gantt.

	Task Name ▾	Act. Start ▾	Act. Finish ▾	% Work ▾	% Comp ▾	Phys. % Comp. ▾	'13 W T F S S M	Jun
1	⊿ **Commercial Valic**	6/3/13	NA	**17%**	17%	0%		
2	Complete com	6/3/13	NA	10%	10%	0%		
3	Finance verify	6/3/13	NA	20%	20%	0%		
4	Commercials a	NA	NA	0%	0%	0%		

4

5   **5**   **5**

	Act. Start ▾	Act. Finish ▾	% Work ▾	% Comp ▾	Phys. % Comp. ▾	'13 W T F S	Jun 3, '13 S M T W T F S S
al Valic	6/3/13	NA	17%	17%	0%		17%
e com	6/3/13	NA	10%	10%	0%		10%
verify	6/3/13	NA	20%	20%	0%		20%
rcials a	NA	NA	0%	0%	0%		6/7

⚠ **CAUTION**   Do not track summary tasks. Their %Complete is automatically calculated based upon the %Complete of their detail tasks.

✓ **TIP**   When the %Work Complete is updated, the %Complete is also updated. The % values seen in the Tracking Gantt chart are always %Complete values.

Setting and displaying the Status Date

The Status Date is the date to which you are updating your project; it's sometimes known as the "as is" date. For example, you receive status updates by email on Friday afternoon, but because of work pressures, you don't get around to updating the project until Tuesday. In order to correctly apply the updates, you need to set the Status Date to Friday, so even though it's currently Tuesday, you are applying the status as of the previous Friday. The Status Date is effectively the demarcation between the past and the future. If the Status Date is set to NA (which it is by default), the current date is used as the Status Date.

The Status Date is used when you update the entire project at once and when the task Mark On Track button is used. When updating a project, it's a good idea to display the Status Date as a line on the chart area; it then acts as a visual reminder when you review the progress of the project.

Set and display the Status Date

1 In the Project tab, click the Status Date button.

2 Enter the Status Date and click OK.

3 Right-click the Gantt chart.

4 Choose Gridlines from the menu.

(continued on next page)

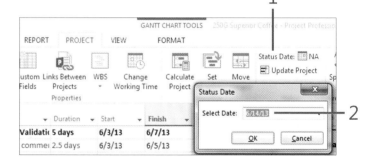

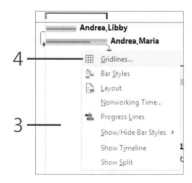

Set and display the Status Date *(continued)*

5 From the Line To Change list, select Status Date.

6 Set the line Type and Color.

7 Click OK.

8 Review the Status Date line in the Gantt chart.

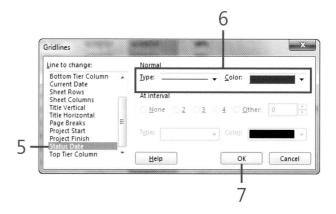

> ✓ **TIP** When the Status Date line is displayed, it's displayed only for the specific chart you are working in at that time. When you change to another view, the Status Date line by default will not be drawn.

> → **TRY THIS** Use the Gridlines dialog box to display Gantt Rows; this is very useful when printing the view on large format printers.

Updating %Complete for the entire project at once

This feature is very useful when the majority of tasks are running to plan because it provides a very quick and effective way to update the status on many tasks at once. Once the majority of tasks are updated, the plan can be "fine-tuned" by updating the minority of tasks that are not running according to plan. It doesn't matter which view is displayed, but ideally you should be able to see the Tracking table and Tracking Gantt.

Update the entire project at once

1 In the Project tab, click the Update Project button.

(continued on next page)

> **TIP** The "Update Work As Complete Through" date will default to the Status Date, and if that is not completed, today's date. You can change this date to a past date or a future date.

> **TIP** Completed tasks are marked as such with a ✓ in the indicators column.

Update the entire project at once *(continued)*

2 Enter the date to update the work to.

3 Choose whether to set anywhere 0%–100% or 0% or 100% only.

4 Choose whether to do this for the entire project or just the selected tasks.

5 Click OK.

6 Review the changes to the project schedule. Tasks are now completed through 6/14/13.

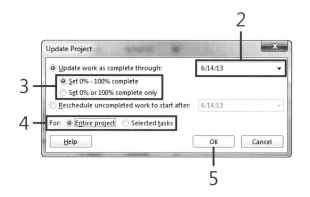

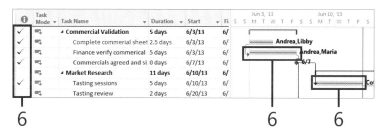

Updating tasks with Actual Start, Actual Duration, and Remaining Duration

Entering information such as Actual Start, Actual Finish, Actual Duration, and Remaining Duration gives a more detailed update than just using % Complete or %Work Complete. When an Actual Finish date is entered, the task will be marked 100% completed as of the entered date. If the work for a task is completed and Remaining Duration is a valid value, zero out the Remaining Duration because the excess time is not needed for the task. If a task needs more time to complete, increase the Remaining Duration.

In order to update the plan, select the Tracking Gantt combined with the Tracking table.

Update a task with Actual Start, Actual Duration, and Remaining Duration

1 Ensure that the Tracking Gantt and Tracking table are applied.

2 Update the Actual Start, Actual Finish, Actual Duration, and Remaining Duration fields in the table for relevant tasks.

(continued on next page)

> **TIP**   Any columns that are not used can be safely hidden. For example, physical percent complete will not be used for the tracking calculations so it can be hidden in the view. The values such as %Complete and Actual Finish date will be automatically calculated.

Update a task with Actual Start, Actual Duration, and Remaining Duration *(continued)*

3 Review the changes to the table and the Tracking Gantt.

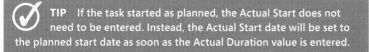

	Task Name	Act. Start	Act. Finish	% Work	% Comp	Phys. % Comp.	Act. Dur.	Rem. Dur.	Jun 3, '13 T F S S M T W T F S S M T Jun 10
1	◢ Commercial Valio	6/4/13	NA	29%	29%	0%	1.43 days	3.57 days	2
2	Complete com	6/4/13	NA	50%	50%	0%	1 day	1 day	50%
3	Finance verify	6/4/13	NA	20%	20%	0%	1 day	4 days	2(
4	Commercials a	NA	NA	0%	0%	0%	0 days	0 days	6

> **TIP** If the task started as planned, the Actual Start does not need to be entered. Instead, the Actual Start date will be set to the planned start date as soon as the Actual Duration value is entered.

Updating tasks with actual work done per period and remaining work

Entering actual work completed per period and remaining work provides a very detailed analysis for the work performed on a project and is similar to the project manager entering his resources' timesheets into the project. This might be too much work, so before you start the process ensure that the time spent collecting and entering the data justifies the way in which you plan to use the information.

To update the plan using actual work hours, use the Task Usage view or the Resource Usage view and add the Actual Work value into the details section of the view.

Update a task with actual work per time period and remaining work

1 Select the Task Usage view from View Shortcuts on the status bar.

2 Click the Format tab.

3 Click the Actual Work check box (in the Details group).

4 Click the Duration column.

5 Click the Insert Column button.

(continued on next page)

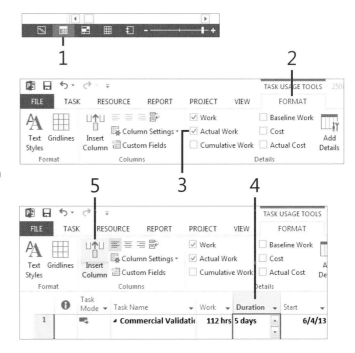

Update a task with actual work per time period and remaining work (continued)

6 Press the R key and select the field Remaining Work.

7 Enter the Actual Work values within the detail pane for each resource and time period.

8 Enter the Remaining Work values into the entry table if necessary.

9 Review the changes to the project plan.

6

7

8

9

9

Rescheduling uncompleted work to a future date

As you track the tasks in your project, you might get to a point where a task was due to be completed but remains at 75 percent complete. In order to represent what should happen in reality, the uncompleted portion of this task should be moved into the future so that the remaining 25 percent of the work can be scheduled. Project makes this very easy for us, and we can complete this task using a few keystrokes. As is often the case in Project, setting up the right view pays dividends; setting and displaying the Status Date goes a long way in helping you visualize the result of rescheduling uncompleted work.

Reschedule uncompleted work to a future date

1   In the Project tab, click the Update Project button.

2   Click the option button Reschedule Uncompleted Work To Start After.

3   Click OK.

4   Review the changes to the project schedule because uncompleted work scheduled before the Status Date is moved to the right of it.

TIP   The "Reschedule Uncompleted Work To Start After" date will default to the Status Date and then the current date if the Status Date has not been set.

TIP   If a task has already started, then rescheduling uncompleted work to start in the future might split the task. This is common during the execution phase of a project. If the task has not started, then the whole task will be moved to start after the date entered in the Update Project dialog box.

Moving tasks forward or backward in the schedule

During part of your planning or project execution, you might want to move a selection of tasks forward or backward in time. This quickly allows you to change parts of the schedule in response to resources who say, "I'll start that in two weeks' time."

It doesn't make too much difference which view you use when you make these changes; however, it's best practice to use the Tracking Gantt to review the changes against the baseline.

Move a task

1 Highlight the task you want to move by clicking the task name cell.

2 In the Task tab, click the Move Task button.

3 Choose the desired option from the drop-down menu.

Amending remaining duration and work estimates

Not only do tasks start late and get interrupted, but also the original duration and work estimates often need amending. Earlier in this section, the opportunity arose to set the remaining work and remaining duration for individual tasks, but I wanted to run through two other options to amend these values.

Extend the duration by dragging the Gantt Bar

1 In the View tab, select the Gantt Chart view.

2 On the Gantt chart, hover over the right-hand side of the bar on the Gantt chart until the cursor changes to ⊢.

3 Click the bar and drag to the right, extending the duration of the task.

4 Review the changes to the project schedule.

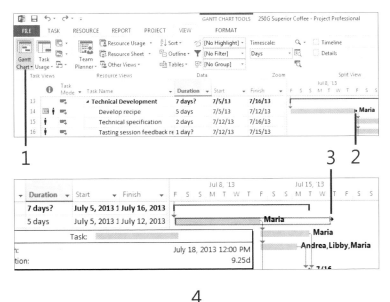

TIP Extending the duration will increase the work value unless the task type is Fixed Work.

Amend the remaining work in the work table

1 In the View tab, click the Tables button.

2 Choose the Work table from the menu.

3 Edit the remaining work values directly in the Work table.

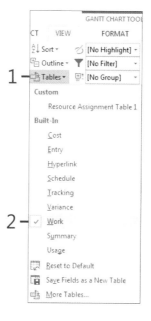

1 —

2 —

Task Name	Work	Baseline	Variance	Actual	Remaining	% W. Comp.
4 Commercials agree	0 hrs	0 hrs	0 hrs	0 hrs	0 hrs	0%
5 ◢ Market Research	88 hrs	88 hrs	0 hrs	24 hrs	64 hrs	27%
6 Tasting sessions	40 hrs	40 hrs	0 hrs	24 hrs	16 hrs	60%
7 Tasting review	16 hrs	16 hrs	0 hrs	0 hrs	16 hrs	0%
8 Feedback to techn	32 hrs	32 hrs	0 hrs	0 hrs	32 hrs	0%

3

TIP Increasing the work will increase the duration unless the task type is Fixed Duration. The additional work will be assigned to the resources at the initial resource allocation unit value.

Closing the project

11

A project schedule needs to be updated during each stage of the life cycle, and this is no less important at the end of the project than it is during the execution phase of the project. It's important to formally close the project in order to tidy up any loose ends and to review any lessons learned so that they can be applied to future projects. Tidying up loose ends involves making sure any tasks that were worked on have zero remaining work or duration, that milestones are set to complete (assuming you achieved them all, of course!), and that any tasks you planned to do but didn't (perhaps due to a change in scope that was never fully reflected in the plan) are dealt with.

Given that at the end of the project you will have spent time fully populating your Work Breakdown Structure, you might want to save the project as a template for future use.

In this section:

- Setting any remaining duration or work to zero
- Setting milestones to 100% complete
- Inactivating unnecessary tasks
- Comparing the final schedule to the baseline
- Comparing different project versions
- Saving a plan as a template

Setting any remaining duration or work to zero

The remaining duration and work for all tasks should be zero. If it's not, you can't fully say that project is complete. Setting any remaining duration and work to zero will also set the %Complete and %Work Complete to 100%.

Note that milestones need to be treated slightly differently (because their duration is already set to zero). They need to have their %Complete set to 100%.

We will use the Incomplete Tasks filter with the Tracking table to view the tasks that are not 100% complete.

Set remaining duration to zero for incomplete tasks

1 In the View tab, click the Gantt Chart button to show the Gantt Chart view.

2 Select the Tracking table from the drop-down list on the Tables button.

(continued on next page)

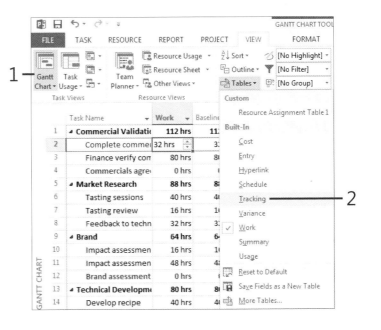

Set remaining duration to zero for incomplete tasks *(continued)*

3 Choose the Incomplete Tasks filter from the Filter menu.

4 For each detail task (that is, non-summary and non-milestone), set the remaining duration to zero.

5 Review the changes to the table and Gantt chart.

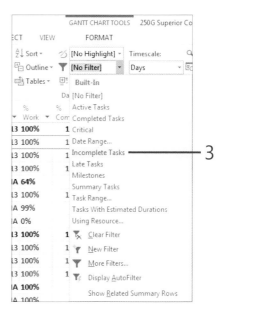

⚠ **CAUTION** Do not change the Remaining Duration value for any summary task or milestone task.

✓ **TIP** To remove the applied filter, press the F3 key or go to the Filter menu and choose No Filter.

Setting milestones to 100% complete

At the end of the project, all of the milestones should be 100% complete. Milestones are often used to represent different key items in a project—for example, deliverable milestones, reporting milestones, and so on.

If a deliverable milestone is not set to 100% complete, this must be due to a change in scope or a failure to deliver the end product. If a reporting milestone is missed, the project might well have achieved its goal but the reporting might have been incomplete. Whether you set each milestone to be complete will depend on what the milestone was used for.

To identify milestones that are not 100% complete, use the Milestones filter and a table that allows you to identify whether the milestones are complete—for example, both the entry table and the Tracking table allow this.

The following are ways to set a milestone (or any task) to 100% complete:

- Use the 100% Complete button in the Task tab.
- Update the %Complete within the Tracking table.

When a milestone (or any task) is 100% complete, the Indicators column in the entry table displays a check mark (✓).

Set a milestone to 100% complete

1   Mouse over the top-left cell in the table to verify that the entry table is displayed.

(continued on next page)

Set a milestone to 100% complete *(continued)*

2 Click the Milestones filter from the Filter drop-down menu.

3 Select the milestone to complete.

4 In the Task tab, click the 100% Complete button.

5 Mouse over the Indicator column to review the change and display the pop-up.

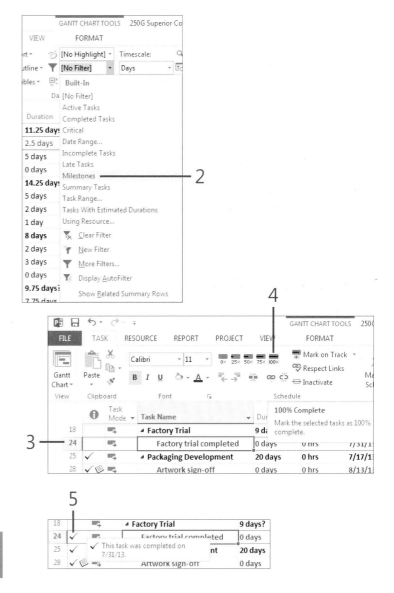

Inactivating unnecessary tasks

Sometimes tasks are planned into a schedule in order to give the project manager a different set of options or to mitigate a risk. For example, if there is a risk that one of the suppliers might not deliver the goods on time, you might add some tasks to the plan to use an alternative supplier. If the option wasn't taken or the risk didn't happen, then these tasks should be set to inactive. Note that the feature to set tasks to inactive is available only in Project Professional.

There are multiple ways to set a task to inactive:

- Use the Inactivate button in the Task tab.
- Right-click the task and choose Inactivate Task from the menu.
- Click the Inactive check box in the General tab in the Task Information dialog box.
- Insert the active column in a table and set the flag to No.

To identify tasks that you didn't need, use the Unstarted Tasks filter.

Inactivate a task

1 In the View tab, click the Gantt Chart button to show the Gantt Chart view.

2 Choose More Filters from the Filter menu.

(continued on next page)

1

2

Inactivate a task (continued)

3 Scroll down to select Unstarted Tasks from the list.

4 Click Apply.

5 Click the Task tab.

6 Highlight the task(s) to inactivate.

7 Click the Inactivate button.

8 Review the changes to the schedule.

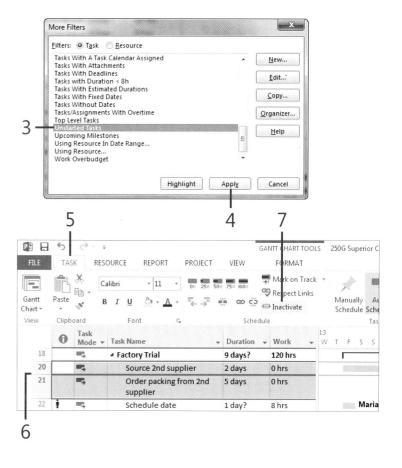

 CAUTION Tasks that have actual values associated with them can't be inactivated.

 TRY THIS Inactivate a summary task to inactivate all the tasks below it.

Comparing the final schedule to the baseline

One thing you can count on is that your final schedule, updated with actual values, will have different start dates, finish dates, durations, and work values from those that you originally planned. The difference between what was planned and what was actually performed (known as variance) is valuable information because it allows you to review which tasks were planned well and performed as expected and which were off plan. Understanding and reviewing this type of information at the end of a project and then taking what you've learned from the project as knowledge to apply to the next project will make you a better project manager!

If you set a baseline at the beginning of your project, you will be able to compare the current plan to the baseline. Project has 11 sets of baseline fields, although a single project can have only one "true" baseline. These sets of baseline data are called Baseline, Baseline1, Baseline2, and so on, through to Baseline10. The variance fields always compare the current fields with the baseline fields—for example, duration variance is the difference between the baseline duration and the duration. The variance fields allow you to easily see how tasks performed in relation to their estimates; common variances used are Duration Variance, Start Variance, Finish Variance, Work Variance, and Cost Variance.

Variance name	Definition and use
Duration Variance	Duration – Baseline Duration
	Used to see the variance between the planned or actual duration and the baseline duration
Start Variance	Start – Baseline Start
	Used to see the variance between the planned or actual start date and the baseline start
Finish Variance	Finish – Baseline Finish
	Used to see the variance between the planned or actual finish date and the baseline finish
Work Variance	Work – Baseline Work
	Used to see the variance between the planned or actual work and the baseline work
Cost Variance	Cost – Baseline Cost
	Used to see the variance between the planned or actual cost and the baseline cost

To compare the baseline against the current plan, use the Tracking Gantt and the Variance table.

Compare the schedule to the baseline

1 In the View tab, select the Tracking Gantt from the drop-down list on the Gantt Chart menu.

2 From the Tables button, choose the Variance table from the drop-down list.

3 Review the various baseline and variance values in the Variance table and the visual representation of the baseline and the task progress in the Tracking Gantt.

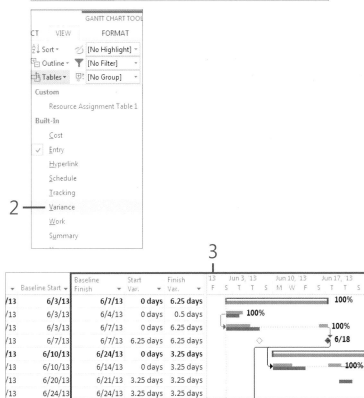

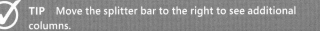

TIP   To add Variance fields into the table, use the Insert Column button in the Format tab.

TIP   Move the splitter bar to the right to see additional columns.

Comparing different project versions

If you periodically saved your project plan as different file names (for example, with the version appended to the file name: MyProjectV1.mpp, MyProjectV2.mpp, and so on) you can use Project to compare these versions and show you the differences between them using a Comparison Report. The

Comparison Report is a sophisticated analysis tool, so set some time aside before you embark on a detailed comparison.

Before you can run a comparison, both projects must be open.

Compare two projects

1 In the Report tab, click the Compare Projects button.

2 Select the previous version of the project to compare to the current project from the drop-down list.

3 Choose the Task Table and Resource Table to compare.

4 Click OK.

(continued on next page)

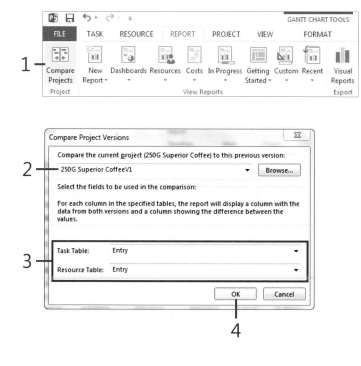

 TRY THIS Save your Comparison Report as a normal plan in order to review it at a later date.

TIP The Comparison Report can be printed just like any standard project schedule.

Compare two projects *(continued)*

5 Review the changes by selecting the items to review.

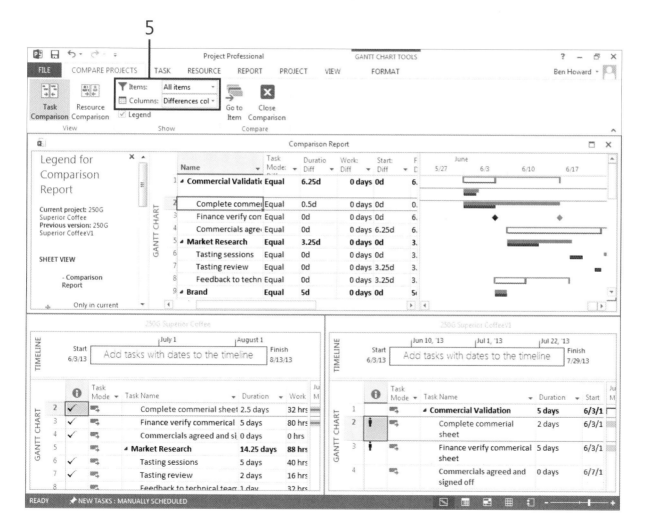

Saving a plan as a template

When a project schedule has been completed, you might want to save the schedule as a template in order to reuse it in the future when you have a similar project to run. Saving the schedule as a template will enable you to create a new project based on a previous project structure.

Save a template

1 Click the File tab to navigate to the Backstage view.

2 Click Export from the Option list.

3 Select Save Project As File.

4 Select Project Template.

5 Click Save As.

(continued on next page)

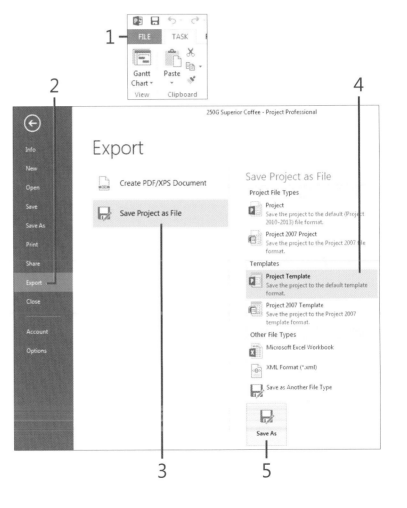

Save a template *(continued)*

6 Choose the location in which to save the template.

7 Enter the file name for the template.

8 Click Save.

9 Select the values to remove before the plan is saved as a template.

10 Click Save.

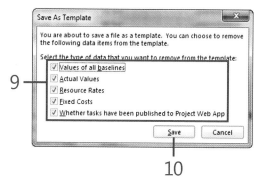

> **TIP** In order to easily save templates to the default location, consider setting the Default personal templates location to %appdata%/Microsoft/Templates within the Save section of the Project Options. Templates that you save there will be available as personal templates from the New dialog box in the Backstage view.

Index

Symbols

24 Hours calendar, description of, 38
% Complete tracking, 177–178, 182, 184, 188
% Work Complete tracking, 177–178, 184

A

account information, viewing in Backstage
    view, 12
Actual Duration, 177–178, 190
Actual Finish date, 190
Actual Start date, 177–178, 190
actual work values, 193
Add A Place option, 167
Alt+Shift+Right shortcut key, 69
Arrow cursor icon, 33
"as is" date, 186
As Late As Possible constraint, 128
assignment-based views, information included
    in, 20
assignment information, choosing correct views
    for, 9
assignments
    default value of, 110
    formula for, 108
    modifications to, 108
assignment units
    adjusting, 114
    defined, 108
    displayed value, 115
As Soon As Possible constraint, 128
Author field, 48
AutoFilter, displaying, 27

B

auto scheduled tasks
    adding external dependencies, 130
    automatic rescheduling of, 62
    calendar exceptions and, 99
    changing start/finish dates and, 126
    and constraints, 120
    effect of new calendars on, 133
    and effort driven tasks, 109
    entering start/finish dates, 128
    estimated durations in, 82
    formatting options for, 143
    unlinking tasks and, 90
    vs. manually scheduled tasks, 181

background color, changing, 138
Backstage view
    accessing, 12
    defining calendar options in, 44
    description of, 12
    exiting, 12
    personal templates, 211
    saving plans with, 53, 167
bars
    formatting all, 142
    formatting multiple, 140
Bar Style, 142
Baseline Duration field, 174
baseline fields, 174, 206
baselines
    auto scheduled tasks and, 181
    basics of, 174

    clearing, 175
    comparing to final schedule, 206
    saving a copy, 175
    setting for entire schedule, 172
    tracking concepts and, 178
    updating existing, 176
Baseline Start field, 174
blue check mark icon, 188
bold command, 138
bottom-up planning, 62
burndown reports
    predefined in Project 2013, 150
    viewing and copying, 154
buttons, description of, 13

C

calendar icon, 133
calendars
    adding to tasks, 132
    and resource assignment, 99, 105
    changing, 39
    defining holidays, 42
    defining options in, 44
    included in MS Project 2013, 38
    setting working week of, 40
cells, formatting, 138
change requests
    discovering implications of, 134
    updating baselines for, 176
Chart area
    description of, 11
    increasing viewing area, 17

About the Author

Ben Howard is a Project and Project Server consultant based in the UK. He blogs semi-frequently at *www.applepark.co.uk/ben-howard-blog/*, holds regular events for the Microsoft Project User Group (*www.mpug.com*), and contributes to Microsoft's Project Forums when time allows. He has been awarded Microsoft's MVP status for the last four years and is the only Project MVP in the UK. His MVP profile can be viewed at *http://www.mvp.microsoft.com/en-us/mvp/Ben%20Howard-4025321*.

What do you think of this book?

We want to hear from you!

To participate in a brief online survey, please visit:

microsoft.com/learning/booksurvey

Tell us how well this book meets your needs—what works effectively, and what we can do better.
Your feedback will help us continually improve our books and learning resources for you.

Thank you in advance for your input!